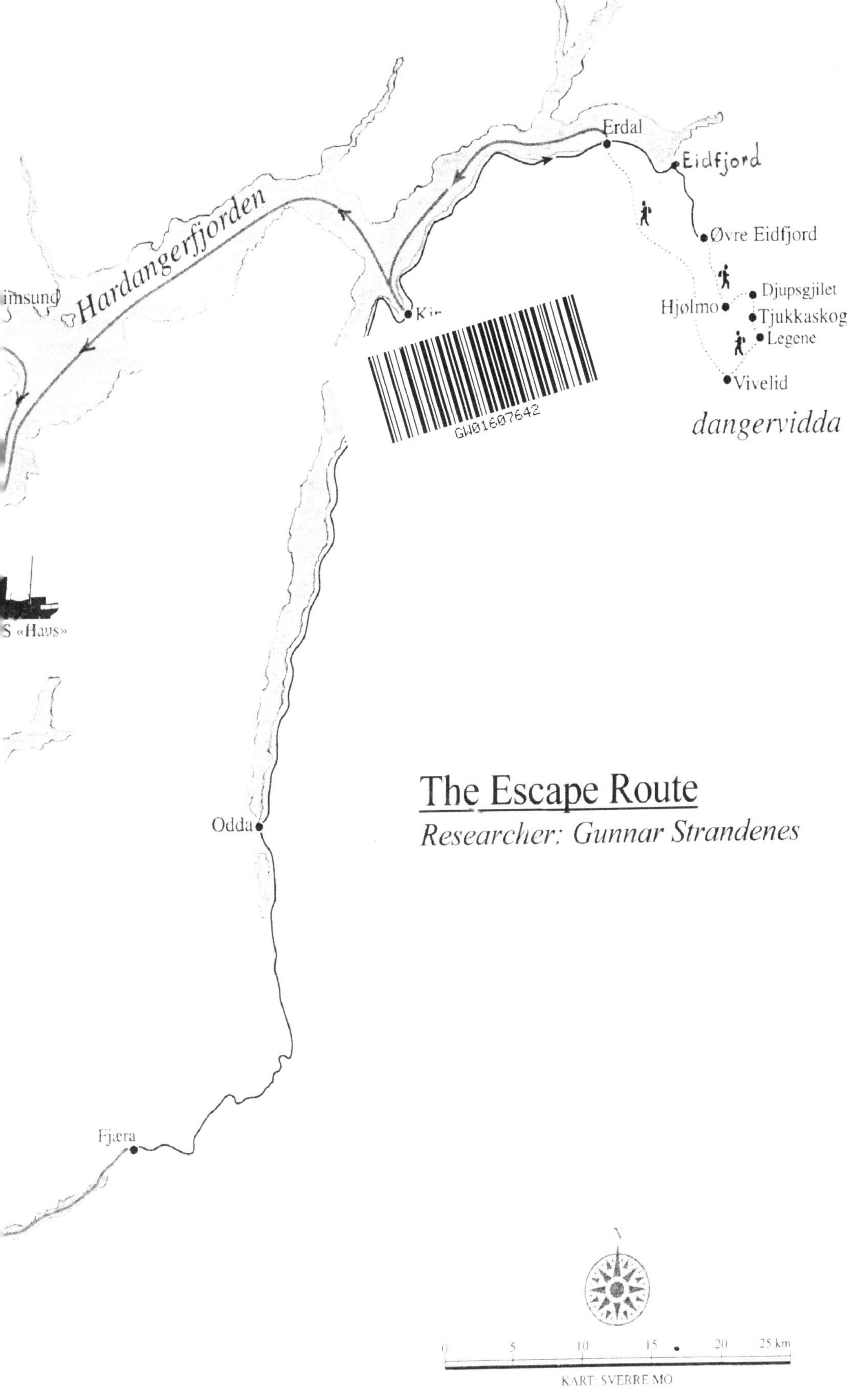
Erdal
Eidfjord
Øvre Eidfjord
Djupsgjilet
Hjølmo
Tjukkaskog
Legene
Vivelid
dangervidda
Hardangerfjorden
imsund
S «Haus»
Odda
Fjæra
The Escape Route
Researcher: Gunnar Strandenes
0
5
10
15
20
25 km
KART: SVERRE MO

HIDING
IN
HARDANGER

This book is dedicated to the many gallant Norwegians of Bergen and Hardanger to whom George Villiers and his family owe their lives.

HIDING IN HARDANGER

The experiences in 1940 of Commander George Villiers R.N. and his family

Written and illustrated by his wife
ANNE HILDA WHELLENS VILLIERS

Finished and compiled by his daughter
JANET MARY VILLIERS

HIDING IN HARDANGER

Published 1998 by
THE PARKFIELD PRESS

Cover illustration
'Building our hut in the birch wood'

Cover design
Liv Jorun Aga

ISBN 0 9532436 0 5

Typeset by Kestrel Data, Exeter, Devon
Printed in Great Britain by Short Run Press Ltd, Exeter, Devon

Chapter One

It was exciting to have a bath after sleeping in our clothes for three months. The children wallowed in the hot water and did strenuous work with a nail-brush someone had left behind in the hotel bathroom, but their feet were so stained by their skiing boots that it would take many such scrubbings to get them clean.

The promise of unlimited baths in the future, and above all the prospect of lunch as soon as we were ready, persuaded them to hurry. The doctor had lent us his room and as the children watched, I began to turn out our damp rucksacks in search of clean clothes.

Slowly the tidy room became rather a shambles as I took out one sorry garment after another. A packet of biscuits, a tin of milk, many pairs of worn stockings and wet packets of cigarettes appeared. These had lately been hurriedly thrust amongst our belongings, but deep down, carefully wrapped about with jerseys and paper, were my treasures which I had preserved. Every night for the last three months I had carefully packed our two rucksacks before we slept.

One held the clothes of my husband and our son Simon, and the other had been mine and our little girl's. Almost daily I had washed our small stock of shirts and socks, so that they were always clean and dry, and so that at a moment's notice we could pull on our boots, pick up our loads and run. The events of the last few days had rather disorganised them, for now most things were soiled and nearly everything was wet. I found a clean, though crumpled, shirt for Simon, and with a tie which had long ago been discarded, it looked quite civilised. Fortunately, there was a pair of dry stockings for him, and those he had been wearing went into the waste-paper basket.

Simon was just thirteen and at the moment looked a typical Norwegian boy, with his knife at his waist, his skiing suit and heavy boots. His face was deeply tanned and his already fair hair bleached almost white by the sun, but now, wet and neatly brushed, it was in good order as I had learned to cut hair on our travels.

There were many odd things which I now added to the heap of clothes which we would not need again, but the small pile of clothes which Janet had left on the floor when she skipped joyfully to the incredible adventure of a hot bath, these I could not throw away. I picked up the grey woollen pinafore dress and cotton blouse which she had been wearing; the yellow wind-jacket with the hood, the long grey stockings and the heavy socks embroidered with reindeer. Nearly all of this outfit had been a present from some unsuspected or new found friend. The dress was made of hand woven vadmel and I had got it from a country woman when Janet's other clothes had become rags. I had cut it out in the snow with my nail-scissors and sewn it with black thread in a large bent needle. The needle, the thread, all had a history. Many times I had blessed the warmth and toughness of this little frock, for it had been soaked and dragged over snow and rocks, waded in and slept in. I could not throw it away.

Apart from our two rucksacks we had with us a very small attache case which had been our little girl's school case. Janet was ten years old when our adventures in Norway began, and this case of hers was little bigger than a toy. Nevertheless, to begin with it had held the entire luggage for four people, and through many vicissitudes it had held together and remained more or less waterproof. Out of it I now took a small sailor-dress. In the breast pocket was a black silk tie, a whistle on a lanyard and two navy blue hair ribbons. It was creased but otherwise like new, for I had only finished making it a few days before we left our home, and I had snatched it from its hanger as we fled. Most small Norwegian girls possess a sailor-dress for parties and occasions in winter, and Janet had at last achieved one, only to wear it once. That had been at our last visit to our dearest friends Commander Lucas and his wife. How proud Janet had been of the Norwegian and British flags prophetically embroidered on her pocket. How happy we all had been and how far we had come since then. Little had we thought that day that less than thirty-six hours later, we with our children would be fleeing, we knew not where, and our hosts would be taken prisoner by the Germans.

'I wish the Lucases were here with us now,' said Janet as she surveyed her unfamiliar self in the long looking-glass. So often our minds travel the same road. The sailor-dress had the same memories for us both.

Out of its wrappings of jerseys and newspapers I now took out my grey suit, which I had cherished for myself, for I had walked away in it that fateful morning, wearing it over another one. It had been carried so many miles since in dark and daylight and it had even served as a pillow when there was nothing else, but I had never worn it. I had folded it carefully several days ago, and now I looked at it with some misgivings, but though creased it was still wearable. I found my only pair of silk stockings and some sport shoes with crepe soles which I had not worn for so long.

As I moved about the room in my new clothes, I felt light and ethereal as if I were wearing evening dress. It must have been nearly two days since I had had anything to eat. I felt thin inside my clothes and missed the thick stockings and heavy boots that I had worn for so many weeks.

Now that we were all ready, we looked at ourselves in the mirror before we descended to the hotel dining room and civilization again. We had had only a three inch mirror for so long that we were indeed strangers to ourselves. Our faces and hands were lean and brown, but we were healthy and happy, and above all, and incredibly, we were alive.

One hour before, we had stepped from our lobster boat onto the quay at Lerwick in the Shetlands. We had stood on the deck of our fifty foot boat while it was tied up to the quay and waited a long time while our passports were examined. We had stood there with mixed feelings as all the formalities were gone through, while the Scottish soldiers looked curiously at us and we had stared silently back at them.

My husband, who with the help of Henrik Platou of Bergen, had found our boat and provisioned it, and then alone plotted our

Stepping on to the quay at Lerwick

course and steered our ship to safety, had soon recognised one of the officers on the quay as a fellow naval officer he knew, and had been the first to step ashore. As he set foot on British soil again he had looked like a large brother of Simon's, for he had lost over three-and-a-half stones in our three months of anxiety. His hair was also sun-bleached, and his face was a deep brown while his neck was strangely thin. He was wearing a Norwegian jersey, wonderfully knitted in natural black and white wool, with antique silver buttons; a red and yellow checked shirt, skiing trousers, red and white patterned stockings, skiing boots, and the inevitable knife hung from the belt round his waist. It was in this same costume that he was flown to the Admiralty in London the next day, and his account of the sensation he caused in these clothes was to make a very good story later.

We had been allowed to land at last, but as we had stepped ashore, I had wondered what would have been our reception if we had arrived without passports. Little did these people know, how not once but many times, we had been on the verge of destroying them; nor could they guess what risks we had taken to keep them.

My husband had been led off at once to make arrangements for the boat (this later became one of the boats used as a 'Shetland Bus') and the two brave Norwegian boys who had come with us, while we were taken by a kindly Captain to the hotel. As in a dream we had clumped through the cobbled streets with our haversacks, while seagulls screamed and wheeled overhead. We had been generously welcomed, given baths and rooms to change in and now we were ready for lunch.

As the children and I turned to go, George appeared in a borrowed dressing gown, and hurriedly began to change into fresh clothes. He had bought a shirt and shoes and someone had lent him a jacket.

As we waited for him and I closed up our rucksacks, cheerful Scottish voices came up to us through the low window. It had been raining, but the sun was coming out. A girl in the opposite window called gaily to a soldier below. A small group of Scots went smartly down the street singing.

Then, at last, did our little family, hearing these cheerful confident sounds, look at each other with beaming eyes, run to hug one another with joy and begin to speak in normal voices again. We had been whispering for so long that until this moment we had not fully realised that we need fear and hide no more, for we were safe at last.

These first moments after our escape when we were almost dazed with relief and happiness are ones which I never want to forget. They are still so vivid in my memory that although they are the end of our adventures they seem a fitting starting point to tell of our experiences. It is so difficult to begin to tell of all that happened to us, for the real starting point shifts every time I try to recall it.

Was the true starting point when we walked out of Bergen at five o'clock in the morning with the German soldiers marching through the streets, or earlier still when we left our home in England at twenty-four hours notice to sail for Norway? Surely before that – the crisis the year before, or even when we left Spain for England four years previously?

It seems impossible to decide, for everything in our whole lives seems to have been leading up to it. For one thing stands out from all our odd memories of danger, fear and exhaustion, and that is the wonderful spirit and a feeling almost of inspiration, which sustained us. We felt that it was meant that we should learn these things. Never had we seen such enduring courage and such goodness of heart than which we found in the Norwegian people who helped us, and never had we been so close or so happy together.

I remember how a few days after we reached the Shetlands, and were once again on the North Sea – this time on a Naval Mail Boat bound for Aberdeen – the children made friends with a young clergyman. He spoke to me during the voyage, in a sympathetic voice. He had been hearing something of our 'terrible experiences', I must remember now, when the frightening part is so uppermost in my mind, that even then I had answered,

'Terrible, yes, but it was worth it. We never knew there were such people in the world until this happened to us. It was more than worth it for the friends we made and the good things we learned.'

We had seen the best of human nature, and my heart was full of gratitude. It must have been a rather startling reply to a purely polite question, but I had not yet descended to the ordinary level of living, and was still, emotionally at least, slightly light-headed.

'That's a bonnie thing to hear,' he had said, 'a very bonnie thing.'

That is not hard to remember – that above all it was a bonnie thing, and truthfully the happiest time of our already happy lives.

* * *

Since then we have come half across the world to Argentina, a country where the war is very remote. When it thunders we remember the bombs, when we hear of the Gestapo in Norway we remember with anguish to pray for our friends, but already time is sweeping past us carrying our memories with it.

For four months now I have tried to ignore the need to write our story. I try to convince myself that there is no need to. It is only one story among hundreds which will be written when this war is over. I invent countless new tasks to busy myself with, I convince myself that I have no time, and when I dwell on our long road to escape, do not my hands begin to tremble and sometimes tears threaten to choke me? The whole effect will be too sentimental, and I shall content myself with a bald account of events. But this plain diary, this is not what is asking to be told! – and once more I tear up what I have written. It was the truth, but so much less than the truth – for it was the little things that mattered, the personal inconsequential things that are important to us. To please myself, to ease myself, I must write it as I can.

This feeling of strain when I recall or talk about Norway is a new thing, for during the actual time for the most part I was calm and controlled. Even in the most hopeless situations we were all controlled and silent; I even began to feel half-ashamed that I did not feel things more. Then, after our first days of shock, it was a relief to look back and to realise that one just did not break down. One seemed to have a hidden reserve of strength to draw upon, and for us there was always the example of the children. They never failed us. Even in our most terrifying experiences the children were helpful and quiet; even when exhausted beyond endurance they staggered on – an inspiration to us and to the guides who helped us.

It seems miraculous that we actually got back to Scotland as we did. Sometimes I think it would have been a more likely ending to our odyssey, if we had never succeeded in our last wild bid for freedom, and if our small boat had indeed been sighted by one of the many aeroplanes, or watch posts that we had to pass, and that we had all perished together. Together, yes, for that we had considered and would have welcomed. For death was not the fear that had haunted us all our long months on the run. A bigger fear had been that at any hour of the day or night George would be caught and torn from us, and as an English Naval Officer be shot as a spy; or perhaps the terrible torture of silence not knowing what they might do to him or where they might send him – or separation from the children. Years of doubt and anxiety would be much more terrible to bear than death.

So we were calm and resolved when we made our final bid for escape. Come what may, we would not be parted. We had even decided that rather than be captured we would take hands and jump together into the sea. It seemed a comfort to have the sea there, so close to us, like a door ajar, inviting our escape.

* * *

Sleepless nights were to be dreaded for one's imagination could not be controlled. In the rare moments up in the mountains when things looked darkest, I would wish that we had a gun, so that should we be discovered by some roving party of brutes, I could shoot the children and myself. It seems incredible as I write this that I ever contemplated such a thing. Sleeping as we were in tumbledown stone huts, miles from anywhere, afraid of every moving speck in the distance – what could have been more incredible than our lives then? – and our fears in the night seemed no less likely to come true. Fortunately we were usually too tired to lie awake with such grim thoughts, and a sleepless night was rare enough to become a thing of foreboding for me, as if my subconscious mind knew that the next day would be a dangerous one – and so it would usually turn out.

But out of all of this, something quite wonderful grew. It was not that because we were in danger of our lives, we valued living more, but that we saw more beauty in life than we had ever realised. The lovely country of Norway had something to do with it, but more it was the kindness and the courage and simplicity of the brave Norwegian people who helped us, at the risk of their lives. They were poor in the sense of the word but they seemed to us richer, in everything worthwhile, than any people we had ever met. They worked very hard, but they had leisure to be kind and untroubled. They had a natural dignity and independence. The way they trusted each other and shared what they had was a continual wonder to us.

This was the way life should be lived. We envied them, and still feel it a privilege that we were allowed to know them.

This then was the happy ending. Telegrams were sent to my dear mother and grandmother and to our friends. My husband flew immediately to the Admiralty with important news. He also delivered two pairs of lobsters especially for the Norwegian King! All the danger was past and I could begin the letter I had longed to write for so long.

'We are saved – our wonderful friends – thank God.' But the letter lay unwritten for many hours. Later, I was surprised and the children almost amused to see the tears falling on the letter.

'You have never cried before. Why begin now?' said Janet, and we managed to laugh together.

Everything was over. We could start life afresh. But everything was over and already so far away. It could never be recaptured.

That is why I was sad.

Chapter Two

DURING THAT LAST SUMMER IN LONDON BEFORE THE WAR began, I spent long hours toiling in our garden. 'Toiling' is the right word, for it was one of my chief pleasures to exhaust myself with quite violent but effective onslaughts. Nothing could give me quite such a satisfactory glow as I felt when I was barely able to stand upright, and surveyed the results of my hours of work.

It was not a large garden, but being on three different levels, it seemed bigger than it was. It had been the kitchen gardens of the old Coombe House, and the tall thick hedges and old walls with their peach trees still remained. We had laid out three lawns, and taken up the ugly cinder paths and made curving grass paths with occasional stepping stones. It had taken three years, and the united efforts of a weekly gardener and ourselves, to get it to look as it did this summer.

We had had years when the whole effect was patchy. I had planted things in the wrong places, and the poor plants had all too frequently to submit to my lightning transplantings, done so quickly, and with so much soil still pressed around their roots, that I hoped they would scarcely notice the change of scene. Even when in flower, they seldom were ungrateful enough to die on me.

Only this year was everything perfect. I found no pansies hiding behind the delphiniums, no Canterbury Bells coming up by mistake in the border edging. Since spring, when the most extravagant array of daffodils and tulips had burst upon us, every

Anne Hilda Whellens Villiers, 1941

plant had flourished and it was as if the whole garden was doing its best for me. I had bought a sack of bulbs as a thanksgiving for the reprieve from war after the Munich crisis, when George had been called up, only to return again after three weeks in Gibraltar. When in full bloom that lovely company of flowers had seemed to express exactly the joy I had felt when I planted them. The very sight of them dancing and blazing in all their bright colours had seemed like a great shout of praise.

That year every day had seemed precious. I valued each phase of spring and early summer as never before. At the first crisis I realised how much I would lose if we had to leave this happy house where we had taken root, and looking back I know I had the nagging fear that this might be for me the last spring – the last summer – there. As things turned out, we never were to see the next spring. It was completely lost to us.

This summer with perhaps some presentiment of what was in store for me, I remember being haunted by the phrase 'Look thy last on all things lovely.' Being drawn indoors to look up that poem, because I could remember no more of it, I began to memorize whole pages of poetry I loved. I decided it was of little use to love so many satisfactory bits of prose and poetry and yet never be able to remember more than a line or two. Lines of Keats, of Francis Thompson, of Chesterton – I learned them as if I were still at school, and I weeded and raked and carted away leaves saying them to myself. I persuaded myself, when it occurred to me more strongly than usual, that I was being rather eccentric, that it would be a good investment for my old age, or should I ever be cast on a desert island; I would have something beautiful amongst the odd jumble of my mind. But the real reason was a deeper, more present one; the picture of our apple trees in bloom demanded some thing more than 'Oh lovely apple-tree!' which was all I could think of, and the roses something more than 'Now sinks the crimson petal' – and the whole quiet garden, as George and I strolled in the dusk, noting every thankful flower that had been freed from weeds, raked and watered – savouring it all, and loving it – how to express it?

Janet would sometimes call from her bedroom window.

'Lovers, can't I come down with you? I can't sleep.' and often we would let her come just to see her prancing about on the grass in her nightgown. Sometimes for a treat she would have a minute

Commander George D. Villiers, R.N.

extra supper with us. Starry-eyed she'd go obediently to bed, knowing it had been a very special day.

* * *

Apart from the all too brief Sunday, these hours in the early dark were the only ones which George had of enjoying our home. We had come back to England in 1936 after having lived all the nine years of our married life abroad. We had been three years in Sweden, and after six years in Spain we had left just before the Civil War. We began a discouraging search for a small house near London, and when we saw our present house, then three empty cottages belonging to the old Coombe estate, we had fallen in love with them at once.

So we bought them – the old gardener's cottage, the laundry with its huge boiler and pipes all round the high walls, and the more modern butler's cottage. After many hesitations and mistakes we had eventually succeeded in joining them to make one perfect house. Perfect in our eyes, because it seemed it would take us the rest of our lives to get it as we really wanted it.

Our furniture, which had seemed a motley collection when it arrived from Spain, had miraculously arranged and settled itself as though it was grateful its wanderings were over. Some of it was Swedish, some Spanish, and some inherited from old English country houses, and a little of it picked up in lucky moments at second-hand shops, but all was warmly adopted by the house.

Gradually it began to have a personality of its own. I would hesitate for weeks before I bought materials, and for some time we grew used to living with strips of odd stuff hanging from the windows or slung over chairs as I grappled for the right colour. I looped frilled delicate curtains at all the windows, made glazed chintzy bedspreads with pleated frills to the floor, made a nursery of dark blue and chalk white with a huge old fireguard, matched wall-paint and loose covers, hunted and schemed for things the house wanted. How vividly I can remember every room even now and feel again the unending pleasure my long task gave me.

It was never finished, and still we saved and planned for it. We used twelve rooms, but there were fifteen altogether, for half the oldest cottage we did not use yet. At Christmas, feeling prosperous, we knocked a large hole through a wall and joined it to our hall,

Simon W. G. Villiers, 1939

and I was planning to move my whole kitchen from one end of the house to the other.

I was lucky in that I had maids who were real friends; one particular treasure, Mrs. Ringshall, entered with zest and skill into distempering and painting. I had had an orgy of repainting in the spring and all the drab painted woodwork was now pale cream. No sooner was one room fresh and dazzling than we would pounce on another, and for days we ate scanty meals and worked until the last moment before the family came home. George and I must have had some mild social life, but what I most remember is the fun I had behind the scenes.

Because George had his own newly launched factory and was working for himself, he worked too hard, driving himself with long hours until he was really ill.

'This is no way to live' we often thought. I saw too little of him, and he was too tired to enjoy his leisure. We would economise in all directions, but still the big house seemed to eat up our income, for the factory was slow in making the success we knew it eventually would. We often used to envy the clerks in his office, earning a small enough salary but having money left over. They would go off for jolly holidays, while we had to contemplate the formidable amount it would cost to take the children and ourselves away.

Only once, two years earlier, we had managed a cheap and lovely holiday. The children were away with their nurse with relations in the country, but there seemed no chance of George getting a vacation. Then suddenly he could manage two weeks holiday, but we could only raise about twenty pounds. Then came the idea that we would go as hikers to Germany – we, who never walked a step, or had imagined a holiday without a car. We left the car in the garage and with a haversack apiece set off rather self-consciously on our trip. It proved the grandest holiday we ever had. It was fun, being poor, asking for the cheapest rooms, yet finding them always clean, and having no luggage to bother about.

We took steamers down the Rhine and Moselle, and walked for miles in any direction we fancied. We met only working people and had memorable evenings talking, singing and dancing in their wine-stubes. We came home with a new repertoire of Rhine songs, and about five shillings in our purse, enthusiastic for the simple life, but we were soon swept back into our civilised harness again. I

Janet M. Villiers, 1939

kept a diary of this trip, with more or less successful drawings of the amusing things we saw. This is probably in German hands now, as I left it in Bergen. I wonder what they made of it?

But this last summer we had no holiday. The children spent joyful hours bathing in the swimming pool of our very charming neighbours. They seemed content, busy from one garden to another, for we were fortunate too in having the big gardens of the old house still around us. We planned to go camping, or to take a motor-launch up the river, but always we hesitated because the clouds of war were gathering again. We lived from day to day. It was a very dry summer and I was kept happily busy watering, and clearing away the dried up flowers. Every day the threat of war drew nearer, and hourly I expected my husband to be called up. As a naval officer on the Emergency List, he would have to be at his post before war began, so as the days went on I began to dread the summons which must come.

The fateful telephone rang that day just as I was about to trundle away the last barrow-load of dead lupins.

'It has come', I thought. 'This must be it.'

As I dropped the handles of the wheelbarrow, and started for the house, I remembered so clearly that other telegram which, almost a year ago at that first fateful crisis, had called me from the same scene – the same happy labours. But how differently I would meet it this time. A year ago I had been unable to take down the long detailed message, ordering George to fly to Gibraltar, because of my shaking hand, and a sympathetic operator had said.

'Take your time Madam, I'll start again.'

This time I was prepared. I expected calamity. Only a few steps through the little smoking-room, and I had lifted off the receiver with my hands still in their earthy gloves.

'Telegram from the Admiralty', said the voice. I pulled pencil and paper towards me.

'So report at once – to leave immediately.'

I wrote it down steadily, while it seemed the whole current of our lives faltered and stopped. Mechanically I made another call to my husband's factory.

'Your telegram has come' was all I needed to say when I heard his voice.

I slowly took off my gloves, changed my muddy gardening shoes, while the realisation of what this meant flooded over me. I

Janet and George Villiers, 1939

must begin to pack at once. I went up to George's dressing room and began a systematic packing of all his clothes: for this much we knew, he was destined for Norway. Last year at a few hours notice he had been flown to Spain, but Norway was better.

'Norway will be the safest spot in the world', I thought gratefully.

I could not finish such a packing in one session, but in one hour there was little more I could do, so I left it. As I passed the window at the top of the stairs, I stood for a moment and looked down into the garden where I could hear shouts and laughter, and just caught a glimpse of Simon scrambling up the rickety ladder and over the high fence. Both families rather frowned on this mode of entry, but it did seem the most satisfactory way of getting there, and saved quite two minutes when exciting things were happening.

The children's packing was the next task on my list, I thought, for they must take mattress, pillows, blankets and clothes when their school evacuated to the country. I still had the heavy straps for their monstrous bundles saved from the other crisis last year. I knew exactly how long it would take me and tomorrow would be soon enough.

I remember so well as I came down the stairs the bright splashes of blue made by my hydrangeas. They were massed three or four pots together in a large copper cauldron on the old chest in the hall, and as I entered the drawing room, there too were more banked in the fireplace and in ivory pots by the grand piano. The house seemed full of them, for I had had a birthday and the family had bought the entire stock of the local florist. I think I had fourteen plants and it had taken me a long time to arrange them. In fact it was a never failing occupation to move them about, and to plant the faded ones in the garden. As I hesitated by my writing desk, I had the happy thought that I would write George a letter which he would find in his collar-box when he was far away from me. Before I sealed it up, I 'rootled' in our snapshot drawer with the intention of enclosing one as a surprise, but as usual I was led on and on, turning over one picture after another – Simon as a baby in Stockholm, the 'beaming peach' the little Swedish children had nicknamed him – and Janet as a baby in Spain with a lovely grin and too little hair. As I turned the pages of the snapshot albums, I was back with my children when they were babies, seeing them as sturdy toddlers, then as serious six- and

Janet and Simon Villiers, 1936

eight-year-olds setting off bravely to their first English school – both of them speaking Spanish as well as English. Handfuls of snapshots, of last year, of this year. I thought then that they were the most precious things I had.

'If there is ever a fire,' I often said – a fire being then the greatest misfortune one could imagine – 'the family snapshots will be the first things I shall save.'

After all, I did not put one in the letter, and it was just as well because George never opened it. It is still in his collar box – somewhere.

When George got home that night after reporting at the Admiralty, we rejoiced because he had two whole days before he must sail. The next day I started the children's packing and, because it was August, I must needs dash out shopping for winter clothes – for Wellington boots grown too small during the summer, for jerseys, shoes and mackintoshes. When at last the bundles were finished and labelled, it was evening and I had had no time to feel miserable about parting from them all.

George had been rushing between his factory and the Admiralty all day. It was Thursday, and he must leave Saturday morning. One piece of news he had. One of the officers going with him was taking his wife and daughter.

'Is it allowed?' I asked in surprise. It had never occurred to us as a possibility before, but now it opened up a wonderful vista. But there were arguments against it. It would take a good deal of money to move us all – we would look foolish if the war did not break out – and there was so little time left.

We had decided against it when we went to bed. It was too tantalising to contemplate, but when Friday morning came, as we drank our early tea, George asked,

'Have you thought any more about Norway?'

'Well,' I said 'I think it would be simplest if we stayed behind.'

'I have quite decided', said my most admirable husband. 'You are all coming with me, if I can only get berths on the ship.'

As soon as George had left I began my own packing and prayed that George would be able to get our passages. At eleven o'clock George telephoned me.

'We got them', he said. 'We leave tomorrow at ten o'clock.'

I needed a few moments to realise it. Then I hurried to tell the servants, to ring up my friends, and extravagantly I arranged for the children to have almost continuous riding lessons throughout the day. They had lately developed a craze for riding, and they hurried off to enjoy the most delightful day they could imagine.

Then I began.

*   *   *

I unpacked the children's bundles, packed into decent trunks everything they had, finished packing all my own clothes, and in the afternoon started on the house. We had a hope that perhaps we might let it furnished while away, so every drawer and cupboard was emptied and ornaments and a roomful of toys moved to one room in the far cottage. All my blankets were stowed away, the silver thrust into felt bags and stacked in a chest. The bright house was denuded of its frilled starched curtains, my cream loose covers were changed for those I valued less. It was like a bleak wind sweeping our personalities out of the house. As the day wore on I had moments when I had to lie flat on the floor to recover, but by nightfall it was all accomplished. We were ready.

I received the friends who came to say goodbye in an overall, with wild hair and eyes like two dark smudges in my white face, but I was radiantly happy. We would be together still. Next morning found us still sticking labels onto our luggage as we waited for the van which was to take it to King's Cross. They must have been very inadequately licked and indeed I was parched with excitement and fatigue, for throughout the journey they curled up and fell like leaves, so that one or two cases eventually arrived in Norway with no labels at all.

At last we had to force ourselves to leave. The servants who had rallied round so nobly promised to clean up the house and swathe it in dust sheets. It only remained for us to give our keys to one of the good neighbours who were waiting to speed our departure, and to take one last quick glance at our despoiled living rooms.

'Well, goodbye House', I called, half apologetically, as I deserted it.

Chapter Three

WE ONLY JUST CAUGHT THE TRAIN TO THE NORTH, FOR WE had to pick up our tickets on the way and consequently spent a nerve-racking time wondering what would happen to George if he missed it. The children decided he might be 'shot at dawn' if he failed to report in time! The station was packed and the train crowded. One beloved college friend, Miss Hunter, had come up from Tunbridge Wells that morning to see us off, and I remember oddly presenting her with a fur coat, a cheese in a little string bag and a complete salami sausage. We always believed in enlivening our English food with any Swedish or Spanish delicacies we could find, and this particular friend had always been a joy to have as a guest, for she would try, and invariably appreciated, such eccentricities; this last gift was really a link with all the happy meals we had had together.

Our luggage had overflowed a little into our arms and Simon was weighed down with overcoats. Janet had had a difficult time deciding what toys she would take with her, for we had stipulated 'only what she could carry herself'. So this morning her little school case was bulging with tiny dolls and treasures, and she hugged her new miniature dolls' house. The teddy-bear, all unsuspecting of the important role he was to play later, was safely squashed into a suitcase, to be released as soon as possible.

Janet had had her adenoids out only four days previously, but as usual looked a picture of health and good temper. How more than fortunate we are that the children were always so tough and healthy, for indeed if they had not been practically unbreakable in health and spirit we should not be together today.

*   *   *

As we left London and its eve-of-battle atmosphere, and the train sped northwards, George and I agreed that we felt like rats leaving the sinking ship. At Newcastle that night we boarded the *Venus*, a beautiful ship that was to take us to Bergen. George was in charge of the Admiralty bags, so that he must have a cabin to himself and arrange for it to be guarded every moment of the voyage. As we explored the ship before she sailed we met the mother and daughter who were indirectly the cause of our own departure, and when the ship got under way we soon made the acquaintance of about a dozen other naval officers who were taking up their posts in Bergen, Stavanger and other parts of Norway. As we went to our bunks that night we wondered if the Germans would already be stopping these neutral ships, and if they knew of the naval officers on board. War was not actually declared until a week later, but at this time we all expected it at any moment.

Next morning was dull and grey and as usual Janet and I felt '*pianissimo*' in the choppy sea. But soon we saw the coast of Norway and from then onwards our passage up the coast, and through the islands, was a delightful experience. The sky was now cloudless, and the sun sparkled on the water as we made our stately progress. We called at Stavanger, and as we drew near to the landing-stages they were always crowded with most of the inhabitants. We were struck by their bright clothes, distinctly gayer than a similar crowd in England; their healthy happy faces and the lovely light-haired children. A few passengers landed at each stop, and it was intriguing to watch the travellers being welcomed by all their friends. So often a very smartly dressed woman, with furs and rakish hat, would totter down the gangway in her high heels to be loudly welcomed by a jolly company of farmers. Pretty, well-dressed girls, tall youths in very long grey or green raincoats, disembarked at every stop and were soon absorbed into the tiny towns.

At Haugesund we had a long wait while chickens and other food were brought on board, and just as we were about to leave the crowd on the jetty, we sighted a car on the distant road, careering full speed ahead for the boat. It was quite exciting to watch the speck growing nearer and finally racing down the village street to reach the quay just as we swung away from it. One felt terribly disappointed for the young couple who gazed after the departing ship. They looked newly-married and I felt quite vexed for them. These towns we passed, from the quay at least, looked little bigger than fair-sized villages, and I hoped but rather doubted that Bergen would be any bigger. The houses seemed charming, built of wood and brightly painted; we had lived in a similar house in Sweden and knew how warm and comfortable they could be, and I was expecting to find the same awaiting me in Bergen.

It is strange how different a real town can be from the picture built up previously in one's mind from one source and another. Although I had visited Norway a few years before when we had driven by car from Stockholm to Oslo, and then back again by a different route, I would be totally unprepared for Bergen.

As on all Scandinavian boats, that evening we had once more a wonderful dinner. There was an endless variety of good things for smørgasbord, and we understood why the chicken and lamb taken on at Stavanger were famous throughout Norway. On this boat we had only paper table napkins, but they were so large and thick and soft, and the only ones I have ever come across that did not shrivel away when you used them.

As it got dark the children and I leant over the rail watching for the approach to Bergen. A Norwegian doctor talked to us as we looked ahead. He was a tall man with a plain humorous face, and he startled the children by telling them that they must eat raw herring and cheese for breakfast every morning.

'Lots of herring and cod-liver oil, or you won't keep strong in Bergen', he said.

'I never eat fish. I don't like it', boasted Janet, but he assured her that she would have to learn to like it if she lived in a town which lived for, ate and talked fish, and had so little sun in the autumn and winter. He was right, and in time we all, including Janet, learned to eat quantities of fish daily.

I asked the doctor where we would find a good but reasonable hotel, and he recommended one that sounded suspiciously like the Salvation Army Hostel. He assured us he had lived there comfortably for months when his house was burned down in 1916.

'That was the big fire in Bergen', he said. 'All the centre of the town was burnt out, and the wind swept the flames right down to the quay. Now the centre of Bergen is laid out with a fine lake and parks and the buildings are large and modern. We have the fire to thank for that, but fortunately many picturesque old houses, dating from the time when Bergen was a famous Hanseatic port, were spared.'

Several hours later our friend eventually summoned us to the rails again, and pointed out the seven mountains which surrounded Bergen. He told us their names and seemed familiar with them all.

'We go long tours all over these mountains when we are boys,' he said, 'hiking in the summer, skiing in the winter.'

As we looked ahead we could see the lighted port at the end of the fjord. As a background, and pressing close around the town, the great dark mountains twinkled with thousands of tiny lights; a great necklace of lights which fell from the sky to the town below showed where the famous funicular ran. It was a lovely sight, and one which afterwards never failed to thrill me – Bergen at dusk! The lighted town was always to have a fascination for me, and so beautiful it was that I scarcely minded the short daylight hours when winter came.

And now, at our first sight of it, as we drew up to the quay and the passengers prepared to disembark, the children and I still leaned over the rails, our eyes not on the milling crowd below, but turned to the pool of light which was the town, to the dark shapes of the ships in the harbour, and always back again to the mysterious mountains.

The air was still and warm but fresh, so that I felt a wonderful sensation of well-being and happiness. I knew then that I had fallen in love with Bergen; I had felt the same instant attraction for a place my first night in Barcelona, but then it had been the thrill of the strangeness of the hot summer night as well as the impulsive sympathy one sometimes feels on a first meeting. Now, uprooted and homeless as we were, how strange that I should feel that I had come home.

Chapter Four

WE FOUND BERGEN CROWDED WITH TRAVELLERS. WAR seemed imminent and people from all over Scandinavia and Russia had cut short their holidays to get home before hostilities began. It was late when we eventually got our luggage through the customs. All the hotels were full and we were lucky to get some cancelled rooms at a small hotel, the Victoria. Mrs. Neat and her daughter came with us, while George departed with his sealed bags to hand them over to the proper quarters.

Next morning, while our husbands reported at their office, Mrs. Neat and her daughter accompanied us on our first walk round the town. It was a beautiful bright day, in fact I had never known such brightness – most newcomers feel distinct eye-strain from it. But this clear light gave the place a startling look and it was with the highest spirits that we walked the cobbled streets to the quay. Part of the quay comes right up into the town and looked like a broad canal with streets of old shops and houses down each side of it. We bought flowers at the market which was alongside the quay and close to the stalls and tanks where they sold the live and still leaping fish. I tried to remember my Swedish, but this first morning I could only produce Spanish, which was not too good! I could see my companions were not too impressed, and soon we found that English produced much better results. We were amazed by the fine buildings in the shopping centre, and by the lovely things in the windows.

At one o'clock a small military band marched through the streets playing a lively air and fetched up in the bandstand in the small park by the lake. Here they played for about an hour, whilst idle people like us sat in the open-air cafe, and workers from the offices and young people from the High Schools strolled down the broad road between.

We soon learned that lunch was never served until two o'clock or half past two, and the afternoon seemed to vanish altogether. At first we chafed against it, especially as we never seemed hungry enough for tea and did not have time to have it at all, but soon we saw the wisdom of it and learned to make the most of the long mornings.

* * *

In England we had left at the end of summer, but here we found ourselves in a summer only well begun. The gardens were full of roses and as fresh as our gardens look in June. It was hot and we soon sought out the bathing-places and made the most of the lovely weather. Bathing in the fjords was a lovely experience for the children. The water was so warm, calm and deep, and so buoyant, that they swam prodigious distances with their father, whilst I who am no swimmer, and behave on these occasions like an anxious hen that has hatched out ducklings, kept an apprehensive eye on them.

One of the officers, Commander Lucas, who had come out with us, now turned out to be a friend indeed. He had left five children at home, and he endeared himself to Simon and Janet by taking them frequently to the movies, for long walks in the mountains and finding new places to swim. Once we hired a taxi and after about an hour's drive, came to a lovely little beach with a fine summer hotel behind. I can see him now, towelling himself vigorously in the sun and teaching a delighted Janet to yodel.

'You're a lay–a–dee', he warbled and,

'You're a lady', piped up Janet fascinated by the way their voices echoed over the water and still countryside.

Later we all ate a great many fallen cherries which were thick on the lawn of the hotel, and returned to town all looking rather blue about the teeth.

Dear Lucas, what has become of you?

We went that first Sunday to the trotting races, where we lost some money; but will always remember that day, because of the news-boys dashing amongst the crowds with a one-sheet newspaper. 'England declares War.' We had expected it, but it was terrible.

* * *

Still in our hotel, George and I developed the habit of taking a stroll after dinner into the town and reading the latest news, written up on large sheets of paper by hand and stuck in the windows of the various newspaper offices. The time when the news was received was always given, so that we would go from office to office, tracking down the latest bulletin. We always learned the most serious news this way. We scarcely bought a newspaper during those first momentous days.

Always the town seemed dominated by the young people who poured out of the numerous schools, and gladdened the streets with their cheerful spirits. At night the whole road beside the bandstand and under the lights of two popular hotels was crowded with these good-looking youngsters, and George and I on our sad errand would feel particularly middle-aged as we pushed our way through the crowd.

After the first week the children began to droop a little, missing their friends and their rather strenuous wild life at home. Simon, now twelve years old, in his English grey shorts and turn-over stockings, felt conspicuous among the local boys. It soon dawned on me that this accounted for his growing lack of enthusiasm for our walks, and one morning he went out with George and bought a real Norwegian suit. It was of brown tweed with a sporty jacket and rather long plus fours. He appeared proudly at lunch wearing some fine sports socks to match, and looking alas, so very much older; but from then onwards we explored more.

We visited the old houses by the quayside, many of them still lived in, and others preserved as museums, but all smelling as they must have done hundreds of years ago. We discovered Nordness Park which is a narrow point of land which juts right out into the fjord, so that we could sit and watch the deep blue water, while big and little ships sailed into the harbour at each side of us. This became a favourite spot for us on a fine day; and for many old seamen too, who would take the air with us, and scan every ship as it passed.

As summer passed, and the first crisp autumn days appeared, it was noticeable how deserted the town would be on a Sunday. We began to feel that except for the babies and the aged, we were the only people left in the deserted streets. We decided that we too, must take a sensible country walk.

The first time we ever did this, I remember we had put on our most country clothes and heavy shoes and with the children had taken the funicular up the famous Floien mountain. Having arrived at the top, and explored the hotel there, which overlooks the whole valley, we had started off with the crowd – and a real crowd it proved to be.

The rough roads were thick with people striding along at twice our pace, and dressed in such a sporty fashion that we felt as if we had made the *faux pas* of turning out in town clothes.

Young men and girls swept past us, in the most attractive costumes I had ever seen. The men with heads thrown back strode along in plus fours and heavy boots with wonderful embroidered stockings and matching cardigans, in black and white and every bright colour from yellow to scarlet. The girls with them looked so attractive, that we felt we must step out of this bright parade and watch from the roadside.

Every costume was different and each girl had spent a lot of trouble on her outfit. I was charmed by their jerseys of red and blue or yellow, their little sleeveless jackets of white fur, and the jackets embroidered lavishly with bright flowers, and always a jaunty cap or bonnet of startling colour trimmed with braid or worked in wools. Even middle-aged women had turned out in their heavy boots and ankle socks, trim skirts and wind-jackets. We had felt so drab and conspicuous and bundled up, that we had gone home sooner than we meant to, and had arrived for our Sunday lunch at 2 pm. Later we managed to dress our children as Norwegians and to pass ourselves in a crowd, and like them we would use all the hours of sunshine and return for lunch at 4 pm.

What a sensible country this, where every little shop-girl and clerk can look so happy and healthy and spend their spare time so cheaply and well. I remember one young man in a draper's shop, with an enamelled badge in his button-hole, offered to take Simon to his club. He described how young men and boys would go out early every weekend for a '*tur*' walking or skiing whatever the weather.

'He must come', he had said. 'He will like it, for many speak English and it is only joyful.' Simon loved it.

* * *

After a month of hotel life we grew tired of it and decided to take a small flat. This was not easy because there were few to be had, and in any case we must wait until quarter day which was more or less official moving day (flitting day). We were very lucky to find a three roomed flat in the most modern building in Strandgaten, the main street. It was five floors up and had a small balcony, and a huge beautiful kitchen lined with big cupboards. The living-room walls were papered, as is usual, with dark brown and orange wallpaper, for the 'towny' Norwegians love a cosy cavern-like appearance in their houses, and to help to get this effect the lights are always mere glow-worms about the room.

We had the wall repapered cream colour at our own expense and while we waited for October 15th I made curtains. I made them of thin net, frilled and looped across the windows as in my house in London. When we moved into our flat we had curtains at the windows, carpets on the floor and nothing else whatever!

Later that day a divan arrived for Simon and a pale green wooden bed for Janet, but George and I slept on cushions on the floor.

We had fun buying large feather beds, which in Norway are used as sheets and blankets and eiderdown combined (duvets). They are wide enough to wrap around you and are the most comfortable bed clothing ever invented. At least we thought so, after a day or two when we had tamed them to do as we wanted.

We acquired a wonderful collapsible bed–divan for the sitting room. The beds fitted one over the other, and by means of a lever there you had two solid twin beds. I made an elegant cream cover for this affair and covered hard stuffed cushions to place along the wall, and we had small book cases made of natural birch which served as sofa arms during the day.

The rest of the furniture was of plain unpolished birch, which after much experiment I used to clean with Vim, and re-polish with white shoe cream.

We had one bedroom for Janet and in case anyone was ill. The room had built-in cupboards the whole width of it and was attractively painted cream and light green. I covered the cheap bed with rose-budded chintz with pleated frills to the ground, and bought a kitchen table which, when it had a bit sawn out of it, I converted into a kidney dressing-table with green skirt and chintz top. The furniture we added was cheap, but when painted cream we thought it charming enough.

We bought the cheapest of white pine furniture for the dining room, and covered the top of the long refectory table with black glass. I made black cushions with bright green cords for the white chairs, and with green glassware on the table, and other odd purchases, we felt the house was complete.

Above all it was warm. As the weather got colder and wetter, it was always a joy to meet such a welcome as the flat would give me. I can feel yet the pleasure which would fill me, when cold from the street I would open the door to be met by a wave of warmth, and by the sun streaming through the windows. That winter I had a huge bunch of honesty set on the window-sill where the light could shine through its transparent leaves. It looked like a little tree of silver balloons and I was loathe to throw it away when at last it dried and fell.

Rain came with the first cold of Autumn, but one was so prepared to be wet that it was fun to go out in it. We had to buy the children long black oilskin capes and sou'westers to wear with Wellington boots, while George too had a long oilskin coat and galoshes. I found a lovely yellow cape and yellow sou'wester and waterproof over-boots and enjoyed going out without an umbrella. An umbrella was practically useless at any time, for when the rain came in earnest, it swept with terrific force down the streets and the wind lashed water up to one's knees.

How often I remember starting off in the heavy rain through the brightly lighted streets to battle my way to the Public Library. I would usually be clutching four books under my cape, and often one of the children, also hugging books, would splash along beside me.

The free library, costing us nothing, was a mine of pleasure for the whole family. Although belonging to such a small town, it had an English section which we never exhausted. English and American novels and biographies of the latest publications filled one section, and with the thousands of other English books on the shelves we felt better served than at our subscription library in London.

The children's section had many books in English which the children were glad to read, and for many weeks they staggered happily under the weight of the old bound volumes of the Boys' Own Paper which they found there. Every evening the junior library was crowded with children of all ages sitting at tables and reading until turned out at 7 pm.

Indeed the library was always crowded and many pleasant hours I spent there, mooching around its shelves in my wet cape and squelching boots.

* * *

It was a great pleasure to see how quickly the children entered into their new life. After a week or two at home we sent them both to school. All the private schools had long since been superseded by the national schools, which offered such advantages that now rich and poor alike sent their children to them. They had fine buildings, intelligent teachers, and free doctoring and dentistry. At Nygaard School, where Simon and Janet went, they had a dental section on the premises with about a dozen qualified dentists in attendance and it did not cost a penny. Even the text books and stationery were free, and although we as foreigners wished to pay something we were not allowed to.

I took Janet to the school her first morning and saw her welcomed by a class of eager little girls and a pleasant round-faced teacher who spoke good English. She felt happy at once for they were uncommonly kind to her, explaining the lessons in English and generally making things easy for her. They soon discovered she could sing and she would be sent from class to class to sing English songs during their English lessons. So she enjoyed her school, learnt new Norwegian songs, went to gymnasium and dancing classes and spent all her free time learning to skate and toboggan.

Simon had started earlier and was soon overwhelmed with friends. School began early, often at 7.30 am but was always over by 2 pm and every afternoon the door bell would ring at frequent intervals and polite small boys would sweep their hats off, bow stiffly and ask in English

'Is Simon at home?'

He would be led off, rather apprehensively at first, to explore the town with these proud small guides and he soon made friends and became like one of them. English must have been well taught in the schools and a lot of enthusiasm for Simon's company was due to the children's eagerness to learn more.

We were all delighted when our friend Lucas decided to send for his wife, and when she arrived and we got to know her, we congratulated ourselves on our good luck, for she was if anything more charming than he. When this happens that a husband and wife are kindred souls it is something to rejoice over indeed, and we properly appreciated our gifts from the gods.

She *was* a rather wonderful person. Small and very slim and active, she was like a caged bird in a drawing room, but in her element striding through the country in the bitterest weather with a map, finding little known byways from place to place, always exploring and altogether self-sufficient. We had some good walks together starting off in freezing cold, taking a bus to help us on our way, and then finding our way home by devious routes. No matter what amount of clothes I wore, I was always cold, and after one such expedition spent nearly an hour in a hot bath before I lost the shivers.

There were about eight English naval officers doing convoy work in Bergen at this time. They were nearly all middle-aged and had been uprooted from their retired lives, but were soon doing an enormous amount of good work. George at thirty-nine had been called up as Lieutenant, but after a short time was promoted to Lieutenant-Commander which made a big difference to our finances.

Every few days a huge convoy of ships would be gathered in the harbour waiting to be escorted to England, and before they sailed George would talk to all the Captains together giving them their orders and explaining the procedure in Norwegian. Always good at languages, his fluency in Norwegian now brought him into contact with hundreds of these fine fellows and he made many friendships among the shipping people who were eager to help Britain. Altogether they sent in convoy – ships, never losing one, and each month these convoys grew bigger.†

---

†This memoir was written during the war, and for obvious reasons some details were not incluced. The names of many of the Norwegian Resistance sadly cannot now be recovered. J.V.

Chapter Five

JUST BEFORE CHRISTMAS THE RAIN STOPPED AND THE COLD weather set in. From the vantage point of our windows in the main street, we watched the exciting preparations for Christmas. Tall cylindrical tubs were placed every few yards along the curb, painted red with dancing dwarfs (trolls), and then little fir trees were planted in them and hung with multi-coloured lights. Looking up the street, watching the picturesque crowd bent on shopping or returning from skiing, the windows ablaze with lights, was like watching a scene from a pantomime. The children were so sturdy and apple-cheeked, and their clothes were so attractive and sensible. Toddlers wore one-piece suits and close fitting helmets of cotton windproof material, and with all their warm bundling clothes underneath, they looked like very solid elves. In their yellow, red and bright blue, they added to the gay scene just as much as did the painted dwarfs and the Santa Clauses in the shop window.

These window displays were a joy, for the Scandinavians have a special flair for window dressing and even a dull shop like an ironmonger's could delight us with its clever symmetrical or bizarre arrangements of tools and kitchenware. Some shops were noted for their window effects, and when they were changed the raising of the curtain was eagerly awaited by small crowds, our family among them.

In this Christmas crowd the small girls looked delightful in tiny bonnets embroidered and tied under the chin, all their fair hair free to frame their perky faces. Short kilted skirts and anoraks with hoods were almost a uniform, but they appeared in such a variety of colours and trimming that I think I never saw two alike.

At the beginning of the cold weather Janet had to abandon her knee length stockings and wear long woollen stockings with short thick worsted socks and heavy boots. Often on coming indoors the children just took off their boots and padded round in their thick socks. When it was cold enough a large playing field was flooded with water and allowed to freeze, and soon the school-children were spending all their free time skating. Janet in her new clothes was soon indistinguishable from her little Norwegian friends. In a tartan kilt, white anorak, tiny white bonnet with red strings, and with her skates in a gaily mittened hand, she would dash off to spend long happy hours on the lighted skating rink. As well as skating Simon developed a passion for skiing and would spend whole days on the mountains with his friends, returning at sundown glowing with fresh air, and a little more expert each day.

It was on Christmas Eve that the first heavy fall of snow covered the town. We had been to a party at the British Consul's house that night and when we stepped into the street in the early hours, a new and thrilling world awaited us. The snow was deep and crackling and a deep blue sky was studded with stars. Blue shadows and the wonderful hush that always seems so startling with the first snow of the year, lay over the world – 'Peace on earth'. As we walked slowly home through this enchanted little town, under this tremendous sky, we felt as insignificant and as humble as tiny black figures on a Christmas card. After a month or two the snow disappeared from the town and fields and soon only the mountains were snow-covered.

* * *

At Easter Bergen was deserted, for all who possibly could had gone up to the mountains for skiing. The next week the town was so full of brown healthy faces that those who had remained behind were conspicuously pale. Signs of spring began to appear in the flower market by the quay. The vendors kept their flowers and potted plants in carts covered with glass, and heated by oil lamps. They had the delightful custom of cutting larch and birch, and forcing out the tender leaves in the heat. I bought bunches of these to gladden our rooms, and with bowls of crocuses, hyacinths and forced hazel catkins around us, we felt spring was really on the way.

One day Simon came home from a trip up the mountains with a high temperature which soon developed into one-sided mumps. He was installed in the only bedroom and duly recovered; six weeks later Janet caught it too. One night when her temperature rose quite high she was delirious for a short time.

'How can we get home again?' she kept asking. 'Such a long way over the sea!' and 'Tell Simon, Simon.' Simon came in and so gently held her hand and talked to her in a tender voice.

'We'll go in a lovely ship', he said. 'It's not far and we'll all be together and home in no time.' It was sweet to see them so – Janet's small hand completely lost in Simon's big one. Even as a tiny boy, he was a person one could turn to and depend on. Janet was soon asleep and much better next day.

The last week in March she was out of quarantine and April 1st saw her once more back at school. We were only to realize later how fortunate we were that we had this illness over when we did, and that the children were well and strong when catastrophe hit us.

Our friends the Lucases who had been living in a hotel now took a minute flat. It was shaped like a fan, all windows overlooking the quay. They furnished it simply, having as we did much fun over the process, and the result was a charming and very comfortable little home. Mrs. Lucas was a gifted artist and had always kept our small colony amused with her humorous sketches of our life in Bergen, and had also made a large pencil drawing of me which gave us the greatest joy, because here at last, where all attempts of photographers had failed, was something my husband would recognise as me. Of all the things we lost, perhaps we regret this most of all.

With the little flat finished, it was quite an occasion when on 7th April we went there for tea for the first time. So this day Janet wore her new sailor-dress and happily started off before us, bearing a flat bowl of purple crocuses, which we had secretly decided matched some of our friend's cushions. There was a young Englishman there, and another guest arrived who worked in the Consulate and had been brought up in Norway and spoke the language with a strong Trondheim accent. When it was time to go, hosts and guests descended into the street – they to go for the always fascinating walk in the lighted town and we to go home again.

'Come and see me soon!' I called as we turned up Strandgaten and met the wind which was always waiting to catch us. The Lucases waved and smiled and strode away towards the quay – he so sturdy and jolly and she so eager and slight beside him. And so they walked out of our lives, for we were never to see them again.

We said goodbye to the Anglo-Norwegian at our door, little knowing that out of the twenty-odd English people on government business in Bergen then, we were to be almost the only ones to reach England again.

Chapter Six

NEXT DAY, MONDAY, I HAD PLANNED TO WASH THE MUSLIN curtains which became soiled so quickly by the smoke from the ships in the near harbour, but for some reason I delayed. There was exciting news that the British Fleet had mined the coast off Narvik, and we were full of surmises as to what this meant or might bring forth. The shopkeepers I met seemed rather apprehensive and one, who sold me a vegetable dish, thought it meant war sooner or later for Norway. In the afternoon a Norwegian friend visited George and with great pleasure and secrecy discussed the news.

'But this is where they *should* have laid the mines', he said and gave George a paper with detailed directions of positions which Norwegian seamen had given him. George of course, had nothing to do with such work, but accepted the information and was delighted with the friendly spirit shown to the British. That night, after the children were in bed, we were loathe to turn off the wireless. There was little news from England, but the Norwegian station announced that ships, believed to be German, were moving up the coast. This was such disturbing news that we listened until midnight when the radio announced that all coastal and lighthouse lights had been extinguished around the coast of Norway; with this news, and the picture in our minds of helpless Norway crouching in the darkness, we went to bed.

We were awoken about 3 am by the sound of distant gunfire.

'What can that be, George?' I said, startled wide awake.

'Probably the Fleet have met those German ships and are having an engagement, miles out at sea', George reassured me. We lay for a short time, each tense and silently listening to the far-off thunder, and fearing our own private fears. The noise began to come nearer and the gunfire became almost continuous, so that simultaneously we decided to dress. What an odd and frightening experience – to dress hurriedly in the dark! My fingers were numb and I began to shake. It was pitch dark and some of my clothes were unaccountably missing. I put on a woollen jersey which later turned out to be Janet's but with my jacket on top it was warm, and with shoes on my feet I felt a new courage.

The children were still asleep, so we went into the kitchen to make tea. We did not dare to turn the lights on, and later found out that they had all been cut off, but now we were grateful for the electric cooker which was an 'accumulative' one, and which automatically stored up heat on the hot plate through the night. We made tea and drank it gratefully, looking down into the deserted street below us. There seemed nobody about, but still the firing went on.

Suddenly the terrific shock of a near explosion shook the building and we heard a call from Janet.

'There's a battle going on out at sea', we told the children. 'You'd both better get dressed.' Then the air-raid warning, which we had heard once before in a practice, began to wail, and we knew that things were nearer to Bergen than we had imagined. Another nervous scrambling for clothes in the dark and soon the children were ready. Loud explosions continued now in good earnest, and we heard the sound of aeroplanes overhead.

It was all so incomprehensible. Who were firing guns? Who were dropping bombs? We could not tell and it was unnerving to be so baffled. Now George gave me a shock.

'I must go and report at the office,' he said 'they may be needing me.'

There were always two men on duty there, and tonight Commander Lucas was one of them. The office was right on the quayside, but it was a round-about walk from our house when the ferry was not working.

'Be careful, won't you?' I said foolishly.

'There's no danger', George said. 'I'll keep close to the houses and come back as soon as I can.'

'Tell Lucas to send Mrs. Lucas over here', I said. 'She must be all alone.' George promised he would and closed the door behind him.

Numbly we watched George go, while the thudding of the bombs continued. It seemed a little lighter now, or perhaps one's eyes were more accustomed to the dark. After our hasty dressing the flat looked wildly untidy, so I began mechanically to put things in order. Janet with her teddy-bear in her arms was now shivering and her teeth chattering in the warm room. I put on her thick furry coat and tucked her up in an eiderdown in a chair. But still she shook, as before. I began to busy myself making beds. I was so feverishly anxious for George and it was a relief to do something. We found some apples and gnawed them absently, listening with all our nerves to the noise, and for George's return. If I had known then to what he had gone, how utterly unbearable the time of waiting would have been – but mercifully I did not know.

At last he returned and with a quick look at his face I tried to guess what news he brought.

'Is it bad news?' I said. 'What happened?'

'Yes, it's very bad', George said and I noticed he looked quite stunned. 'The Germans have landed. They are in the streets.'

* * *

There seemed nothing to say. It was too incredible. At this moment we were dazed; George told us a little of what he had seen, but not the whole story. I only learned that many hours later.

He had gone through the streets down to the quayside towards the office. It overlooked the water, and as he turned in at the door he had seen soldiers standing about near the boats. As he entered the office and met three of his colleagues he had remarked something to the effect that 'the Norwegian army seemed to be about, anyway'.

'Those are not Norwegians', one of them replied tersely, 'they're Germans.' And looking from the window George had seen that indeed this was true.

They had feverishly begun to destroy documents, but with the Germans a few yards away from their door, and obviously about to raid them any moment, the Captain advised the more junior officers to get away if they could. George walked out with

Commander Hogg, and together they had walked with and through the German troops along the quay to the town. Here they parted and George reached our flat without being stopped.

Fearfully I rushed to the window expecting to see guards outside the house, for without doubt the Germans must know the whereabouts of all the English convoy officers. We can only surmise that the reason they did not come at once must have been that the men detailed for this job were killed in the fighting that took place before they landed.

While we were standing numbly trying to think of some plan of action, two people arrived at our door. They were a Paymaster and his Russian wife, Mr. and Mrs. Stoddart, who lived close by, and they had had a good view of the excitement around the German Consulate from their window. Alarmed by the sight of uniformed German soldiers there, and by the now heavy bombing, they had come to us, their nearest neighbours, to hear what we were going to do. He had not gone to the office, but by telephone had been told to get away if he could.

We did not know this couple very well, but liked what little we had seen of them. He was a long thin quiet man who had spent many years in Russia and Latvia, and had recently married his Russian wife, who was completely his opposite. Small, plump and voluble, she could be very charming and amusing at a party. They were both previously divorced and had grown-up children.

Only twice in all our adventures did I ever influence our movements: each time it was as now, feeling a tremendous urge and conviction that we must flee; that any place would be safer than the present one, and we must get out of it at once. At first I urged the men, at least, to go, and perhaps somehow, somehow we could join them later. But where to go? That was a problem. Our visitors had no suggestions to offer and knew no-one who might help. Neither of them spoke or understood Norwegian, their common languages being German and more seldom, Russian.

George remembered a Norwegian who lived some short distance out of town. He was friendly to the British and George had done him a trivial good turn now and then.

'If we could get there for a start', George thought, and decided to borrow a telephone from someone in our building. He hurried off at once to try this rather forlorn hope. Meanwhile the bombing continued and for safety we others decided to descend to

a windowless corridor on the third floor while we waited for George to come back.

'Come on Simon!' I called as we prepared to leave, but he was not to be seen. We discovered him at the kitchen table eating a hearty breakfast of fried eggs, bacon and sausage, which he had cooked himself. Reluctantly he had to forego his bread and marmalade, and we all made our way downstairs.

After sheltering here for a few minutes, I thought frantically of all the useful things left upstairs that we might want. Simon had no coat. Janet unaccountably was wearing Wellington boots. I slipped up the stairs two at a time, and into the flat. I found Janet's small school-case full of books and emptied it wholesale onto the floor. Desperately in the noise I wondered what to put in it. I snatched up a pair of Janet's shoes and the case was almost full. A silk nightdress for me and one for Janet – my powder box and a comb – I stuffed two pairs of stockings in a corner and looked wildly at the long wardrobe and shelves, filled with clothes and fortunately a picture of neatness. The sailor dress I had just made would just fit on the top of the case. I squashed it in and ran down to the third floor again.

Our friends were still there and the children seemed to have got over the shock and were chatting cheerfully. After a moment or two, and seeing the children were all right, I began to think longingly of other things I had left upstairs. I was wearing a tan tailored suit, but had a newer grey one and a fur coat which I was loathe to lose – and then our passports! I *must* get them. Up through the noise I dashed again, Simon with me, and met George at the door.

'It's arranged', he said. 'We can go there at once.'

We entered the flat together and I got the passports and then began rummaging in a dazed fashion in a drawer. George spied a little jewel box and he slipped it into his pocket. I put my fur coat and grey suit over my arm, Simon got his raincoat and we walked out of our house for the last time. We rejoined our friends on the third floor, and as I put on my extra suit and my fur coat, George told them his plans. They wished to come with us and take a chance, so we set off together. I asked them as we descended the stairs if they had their passports, for they had no luggage whatever, and Stoddart hurried ahead to get them. We reached the ground floor where a group of women with white worried faces were standing talking in low voices. We did not speak to those we knew. Already we felt homeless, set apart.

We opened the street door and prepared to step outside into the chill early morning air, and just at that moment a detachment of German soldiers, four or five deep, spreading out over the road, marched past.

'It's too late', we whispered to each other and drew back into the shadow. George urged us on.

'Don't speak. Not even a whisper,' he said, 'and keep straight on.'

We stepped out into the grey morning. It must have been about 5.30 am and there were few people in the streets. For a few minutes we walked side by side with the soldiers, but they were marching smartly and soon left us behind. We walked shakily on, and Stoddart, returning, joined us without a word.

The Germans were marching to the Post Office to take over the telegraph and other buildings. We silently followed behind them.

"We spread out up the road in twos"

Janet and her teddy bear and I leading, Simon with his father and our friends behind. When we came near the Post Office, with no appearance of hurry, we turned down a side street. (We had seen a man being roughly thrown out down the PO stairs by some soldiers.) Then by round-about ways we reached the high road which led out of town. So far we had passed only small groups of Norwegians anxiously talking together, or parents with children and suitcases making for the station. As we began to climb the hill of the main road, cars and taxis began to pass us in every increasing numbers. At breakneck speed they rushed into town or out towards the country; who they carried we could not guess, but none were empty or looked willing to give us a lift.

As we walked silently on we passed churches and buildings where already the Germans had posted notices in Norwegian. We had no time to read in detail, but it was clear that they had been printed at leisure and that they told the people to be calm, for the Germans had only come to protect them from the British.

After three-quarters of an hour we reached the house which the British Consul had moved into only six weeks ago. We had passed it by only a few yards when the Consul's wife ran out and called after us. She looked terribly shaken, which indeed we all did, but she begged us to come and have coffee with her. But we only wished to get away while we could, and to her question of where we were going we said that we did not know, but meant to hide if we could. So we pressed on, and continued our grim walk, feeling a desperate need for hurry.

(It is interesting to know now that but for the German's delay in finding the Consul's new house, we could never have passed up this road. We learned later that the Germans had the old address of the consul and had gone there to find him. We had slipped past his unguarded house while they were finding out their mistake.)

After walking for some time we began to look for the address we had been given. We had only a vague idea where it might be, for this, our first friend in the strange world into which we had been thrust, was known only in a business way by George, and yet without hesitation he had offered to help us. George had left us to look at the names of streets, and we others were standing waiting for him when a car going at a good speed pulled up with a jerk beside us. In it were two Norwegians, unshaven and still wearing their nightclothes under their suits and overcoats.

'Are you Villiers and Stoddart?' one of the men asked in Norwegian. I looked at the others.

'Yes', I admitted, being the only one who could speak the language.

'The Germans are looking for you', they said.

With only an hour out of town this was bad news indeed. These men had just called in at the Consul's to warn him and I suppose he had sent them after us to warn us. With such urgent need for haste I boldly asked them if they would lend us their car or drive us to the next town only five or six miles distant. They stubbornly refused, with many different excuses, for obviously they thought it too risky. However, when George rejoined us and talked to them, they relented, and offered to take us to the street we were seeking. It was a long street and we did not mention the number. They too found it difficult to find, and it was while we were anxiously heading towards town again in our search that Stoddart saw the Captain striding along alone, evidently bent on walking to escape into the hills. He had lived in Norway over seventeen years and could pass as a Norwegian. With our ill-assorted party it was a different matter.

We had to retrace our way many times before the car finally set us down near the street we were seeking. We thanked the men with real gratitude and sought out the house. As our host opened his door to us, and invited us inside, I was afraid for the danger we might bring upon him, yet with relief we saw the door shut behind us.

For a short time at least we would be safe. We had time to make plans. The lady of the house now welcomed us warmly, and produced a fine breakfast which I for one, could not swallow, but some of us managed to eat a little. Two charming children pressed us to eat, while their father telephoned continuously for some sort of car for us to get to the next town. We had time to wash and tidy ourselves, but even make-up could not hide our ghastly paleness. I took off my fur coat; I still had my two skirts and two jackets underneath it, and at last I was beginning to thaw.

After about half-an-hour at the telephone our friend announced that it was impossible to get anything to take us away. He had tried everything he knew, but there were no cars to be had. It seemed hopeless; we had come so far safely, but it seemed we must go back again before we got these good people into trouble. I remember at this point going off to the end of the room with George, and for both of us it was a poignant moment.

'It looks like the end', George said, 'and I can't bear to leave you like this.' That moment of despair passed and we prepared ourselves for the worst.

At this point our host suddenly bethought of him an Englishman he knew, a Mr Eric Welsh. We had never heard of him as he was a business man resident in the country many years, but our friend began to telephone once more. Then events moved quickly. Mr. Welsh promised to come and fetch us in his car. There seemed to be a path opening before us again. We waited hopefully now, but with a terrible feeling of impatience and dread.

George and Stoddart had very little money on them, but they now wrote cheques and borrowed as much as they could. We waited so long that we feared the car would not come after all. There were still distant explosions, and the sky was full of aeroplanes flying low over the town. The menacing drone of their engines and their low altitude were obviously meant to intimidate the inhabitants and to proclaim without a doubt that the town was in German hands.

'Surely,' we thought, 'all roads leading out of town must be picketed by this time.' Yet still we were anxious for the car which would help us make a dash for it.

At last the son of the car owner came and said his father would soon bring the car. They had been busy burning papers since dawn. Shortly after, his father appeared and seemed surprised that we were not the Consular party that he had understood he was to take, but he consented to drive us and packed us all into his car.

After expressing our deepest gratitude to these fine people, whom we hoped would not suffer for their kindness, we started off, and joined the stream of traffic making for the next town. As we travelled along, the men discussed what we should do if challenged by German soldiers – whether to try and pass as Norwegians or to give ourselves up. We had still not come to any decision, and had rather decided to trust to the inspiration of the moment, when we reached the outskirts of town.

The traffic was thick and we moved forward slowly until we came to a standstill in a traffic block in the main street. The place was packed with the inhabitants watching the cars, and the congestion was soon made worse by the appearance of a small force of Norwegian soldiers, each man leading a horse and transport carriage. They passed us, going in the direction of Bergen and we thought mistakenly that they were going to surrender there. Inch by inch we moved forward, our feelings numbed. We could only wait and pray in our hearts. We crept through the town and coming to a crossroads turned onto a road leading to the left. Then gradually we were surprised to realise that we were actually out of the town and driving into the open country. There had been no search party holding up the traffic. Clearly we had beaten the Germans to it and once more had another chance to get away.

As we drove along we now began to look out for another car to take us further on, for our good friend must go back for his Norwegian wife and children. We only now realised how very good he had been to bring us so far, when he must go back again to fetch his own family. We stopped several empty taxis, but they would not take us. As we were driven reluctantly on, Janet succumbed to car-sickness and fright, and I had to get out and hold her head by the roadside. At last a passing car agreed, for a good sum, to take us up to snow-level and gratefully we climbed in. We waved goodbye to yet another fine friend, little thinking that we would meet him again the following day.

He told us then, but it is fitting to tell it here, what happened to him when he left us. Entering the small town again, which we had left twenty minutes before, he found Germans in charge and stopping all cars from the town. Considerably frightened he had parked his car in a side street and then sent a taxi into Bergen for his family. After a long anxious wait they had arrived, and being obviously Norwegian had been allowed to pass, and had then been successfully brought to his car in the quiet street. They had driven off at great speed to the road and the mountains, brushing into a large lorry as they passed, but fortunately getting away safely.

Once more by the narrow margin of a few minutes we had escaped. Although we did not know at this time how close we had been to arrest, as our car got further and further away from Bergen, our spirits rose and Janet even burst into song. We still had to stop once or twice for her to be sick, but we were all so relieved to see the lovely snow-clad mountains, and to be away from the firing and the aeroplanes.

'Surely,' we told each other, 'the Germans will not attempt this road today.' They would have enough work to keep them in the town and the British would certainly be making an attack soon, which would keep them in Bergen.

'It's a hap–hap–happy day!' sang Janet, and our driver chuckled and chatted to us in a very friendly fashion as he drove us higher and higher up into the snow.

But our thoughts returned again and again to the friends we had left behind. How we wished the Lucases were with us. The children were clearly worried about them. Now we know that only our prompt decision to walk into the street saved us. All the other officers of the Convoy Office and Consulate were arrested and interned, all except us and the Captain whom we were to meet many weeks later when we were still in hiding.

George had now the whole responsibility for this party on his shoulders, for he alone could speak convincing Norwegian. The children and I spoke adequately enough, but our two friends nothing whatever. George had a difficult job ahead of him with such a large and ill-assorted party.

Chapter Seven

AFTER DRIVING FOR ABOUT THREE HOURS, WE CAME AT LAST TO deep snow-covered hills, where the 'Bergensker' would come for their skiing. We reached a small tourist hotel which our taxi driver recognised, and there we got out, sinking up to our knees in snow. Our driver promised me not to speak about bringing us there, and well satisfied with the money we paid him, he turned back to the town.

Careful of the snow in our unsuitable foot gear we went up to the house, where George asked the woman who opened the door if we could stay the night. She invited us in, and we entered an icy cold house which had clearly no expectation of visitors. She had heard the firing and bombing in distant Bergen, but our news of the German landing was news to her. We were given bedrooms and maids rushed in and quickly lit the wood stoves, which in no time at all had the rooms warm. Janet and Simon and I lay down and rested in our underclothes, while George talked with the people in the hotel and studied a small map which he found there.

We did not sleep, but when a lunch of fish was served at 2.30 pm we were rested and ravenously hungry. Quite a number of other guests had now arrived from Bergen, a woman with a baby with only one shoe and two other small children and several men. We talked very little, thinking it wiser for them to consider us Norwegians like themselves and not the hunted fugitives we really were.

After lunch George, Stoddart and Simon ordered a rickety car to take them to the next village, for now our greatest need was to acquire warm stockings and thick boots. While they were away, Janet and I joined Mrs. Stoddart by her stove, and she began to tell us of some of her awful experiences as a refugee in Russia twenty years before. When I saw Janet's eyes getting too round we went off to rest once more and rather longed for the sound of the returning car.

After some time Janet went out into the snow to reach the outside toilets when she could find none inside the hotel, and later came back with only one Wellington boot. The other had been sucked off in the deep snow and now, firmly frozen, resisted all attempts to pull it up.

Just then we heard the welcome sound of the boys returning, and Simon and George between them managed to retrieve it. They were laden with parcels. Heavy boots for Simon and George, woollen socks and stockings, toothbrushes and handkerchiefs.

Just before six o'clock George and I set out to try and find a radio, for we were anxious for news. We had been directed to a little house not far away, and after clambering up a slippery hill we reached the door. The tiny living room was almost full of people listening to the news from Sweden. We too listened and heard that Oslo had fallen into German hands after a short fight. On hearing that we wished for the English news, these kind people directed us to another house further up the road, and thanking them we slid and stumbled down the hill again. How unreal one felt as one walked along the road through the white deserted countryside. I remember how dry my mouth was and how my head felt hot and light as if I had a fever. We reached a bigger house, and the large owner who invited us in was listening to the end of the English news as we entered. But we were really too late to learn anything and after talking for a while, the man invited George to come over and listen to the nine o'clock broadcast.

As we retraced our steps we saw a little kiosk by the roadside, so we stopped and bought oranges and chocolate there. We had learnt very little of what was happening in Norway. The Norwegian radio had been promptly taken over by the Germans; there had been many ships sunk on both sides, but there was no news of a British landing anywhere. We pored over the map for hours, seeking inspiration for a plan of escape. We could have hurried on deep into the country, but if the British made a landing on the coast, we would only be further away from rescue. The little village by the fjord, which we had visited that afternoon for clothes, seemed a likely place for a landing, and perhaps it would be wiser not to go too far away; but before going to bed we ordered a car for the next morning for eight o'clock. We decided after all that we would feel safer if we were further from Bergen. George and Stoddart went out again at 9 pm, but brought back little news to comfort us.

* * *

That night I slept little, for lorries and cars, full of children and refugees, sped down the road until dawn. I felt that we too should have joined that procession, and that we had wasted valuable time in staying the night. At about 3 am a car stopped outside the hotel and two men walked up to the door and proceeded to hammer on it until it was opened. I heard them talking downstairs and lay in fear, hesitating to wake an exhausted George, and feeling certain that we had been traced and that these men had come for us. But as I lay there, almost too frightened to breathe, time passed, and at last, no summons being forthcoming, I eventually dropped off to sleep.

We were up early and waiting for our car long before it appeared. When at last it came, we climbed into it eager to get on, and our spirits rose as we put more and more miles behind us. The road was in a very bad state from the traffic the night before, and the old car slid and bounced from side to side of the rutted road. Worse still was to come when the road led over a high range of mountains. It was cut out of sheer rock, and twisted and curved for several miles with a drop of hundreds of feet on one side. As our car skidded and rushed round the corners, we admired the lovely long blue icicles, the beautiful valley, but more than half our minds were terribly aware of the all too near edge of the road and the drop below. At last we came onto a straight road and after a short drive came into the town of Norheimsund which lay at the head of a fjord.

There was no snow here. The place was seething with activity, and cars were parked thickly along the road. Refugees from miles around had congregated here, and the young men of the town had been hurriedly called up for the army that morning, and had just left by boat when we arrived. George and Stoddart now went off to find the mayor and police of the town, thinking it would be safer to report to them, and hoping that they could, by revealing their identity, borrow some money.

While they left us in the car we caught sight of Mr. Welsh who had helped us the previous day, and with him we went to the big Sandven Hotel to wait. He told us of his adventures, and as he smoked and talked his hand trembled as with cold. This would happen to all of us now and then. Since the first shock of that terrifying gunfire, we had all known moments of acute trembling, when our knees seemed to melt and shivering shook our whole bodies, but only our hands and white faces betrayed us. These moments would pass as suddenly as they came and one would be left feeling strangely calm and empty, but untroubled again.

Our husbands returned to the hotel having had no success at all, and we had a welcome meal together in the very crowded dining room. People thronged the public rooms and cars loaded up and drove off continuously. These people had somewhere to go; we had no idea what to do. Mr. Welsh told us that the hotel proprietress was very sympathetic towards the British and George decided to find her and ask her to help us.

He found her frantically busy with hundreds of guests suddenly descended on her hotel, but she readily listened to him. This Fru Sandven, who we will always remember with gratitude, was a small fair person, a leading spirit in the little town and a woman of character. She was carrying on her fine hotel after the death of her husband some years before, and she had three practically grown-up children, one girl at present in Oslo.

George came back from his long talk with her very much cheered, for she had promised to arrange some plan for us and meanwhile we could buy skiing clothes and other necessities at her shop adjoining the hotel. To enable us to do this, George had produced my small array of jewellery, which was worth perhaps 200 pounds, and had left them with her to pay for them. I was still wearing a valuable diamond ring and George had a fine watch, the possession of which was always to be the greatest comfort to us later.

Now, we all, the Stoddarts included, invaded the small shop, which was doing a roaring trade, and hurriedly bought trousers, boots, stockings and jerseys. There were so many shoppers that the whole process was rather a scramble. As we were trying to find things to fit, I was suddenly aware that people were looking rather curiously at us. In the excitement of choosing their outfit, Mrs. Stoddart and her husband were talking unrestrainedly in German! Though we did not know it, several people had hastened off to inform the lady who had promised to help us, and to warn her. All unsuspecting I collected clothes for the children and myself, while George tried in vain to get more than one shirt which would fit him. When we had finished our friends' bundles cost more than twice what we had spent on the four of us. It was an odd sensation buying in such a wholesale fashion. The cost hardly mattered for I never expected to see my jewels again; but we could not get far in our present inadequate clothes and needed some money left over.

After lunch George had another long talk with Fru Sandven who told him that the hut she had considered lending us was on second thoughts not suitable, and we were a little dismayed that she did not seem so eager to help. Many days later she explained to us how disturbed she had been on hearing our companions speak German, and how her friends had warned her against having anything to do with us. Yet in spite of this, when after several hours George besought her again she said she had another hut, more deeply hidden away, to which we could go.

We waited for a long time watching the last guests leave, and wishing we too were on the way to somewhere. At last Fru Sandven told us that she would arrange to have us taken to the hut late in the afternoon. It was some distance from the high road and she thought we could hide there, but we must promise to lie low. The hut, she said, was being prepared for us now, and as soon as our shopping for food was done, her son would drive us.

What a lightening of the heart we experienced on hearing this promise! We tried to express our gratitude for her sympathy and kindness, and went to tell the others what had been arranged. We made lists of what we should want and in different parties set out to buy. It was a lengthy business and it was late when our packages were finally all stowed in the car which waited for us. I made one feminine expedition with Mrs. Stoddart, buying postcards of the town and the mountain road. She wisely bought two packs of playing cards and I stocked up with cold cream, pencils and paper and other odds and ends. George came back with a bottle of medicine for me which he had been at some trouble to get. I had lately been rather fading away in Bergen and this tonic had been prescribed by a doctor there as an experiment as he could find nothing wrong with me.

When we climbed into the car it was already beginning to get dusk, but we congratulated ourselves on having some roof to go to. The car started off and it was rather disconcerting to realise that we were once more on the road we had travelled that morning and heading again for the dreaded mountain pass in the direction of Bergen. At the foot of the mountains we stopped a long time while a youth who accompanied the driver got out to fetch the key. He had to climb up the side of a waterfall and was out of sight for half an hour. When he appeared again, hot and muddy, he announced that, after all, we would find the key at the hut, so we started again.

With, in the women of the party at least, sinking hearts, the car took the mountain road again, and for the second time that day we clung to the side of the car and to each other while the car lurched along. The snow had turned to mud and slush and frequently the wheels refused to grip, and the men had to get out and push.

After a few experiences of the car slipping and sliding almost to the edge of the precipice, Mrs. Stoddart said she would rather walk. Janet and I found her nervousness catching and we were glad to get out with her and to feel firm ground under our feet again. We started off walking in the dusk, while the men and Simon stayed with the car to help haul it out of the mud when it stuck. We walked on, far out of sight of the car that laboured behind us. It was rapidly getting dark and the road was silent and deserted. I really could not help laughing when I thought how pathetic and comic we must look and how unreal and utterly fantastic our plight was. We strode along quite cheerfully, Janet even doing an extra bit of running like a puppy taken for a walk. She delighted in tapping the enormous icicles which sang out musically. Sometimes the car passed us, and then we would catch them up again while they heaved and pushed.

As it got darker and our temporary good spirits rather deserted us, the men walked along with us. We must have looked pathetic to them with Janet trudging with us carrying her teddy-bear. In this fashion we walked the entire way until we came to the straight road again. It was now getting darker and we hastened to catch up the car which was waiting for us further up the road. It was surrounded by people in skiing clothes, who were obviously staying at the small hotel near the road. As we shyly got into the car, a man stepped forward and asked me if we were English. On learning we were, he offered to help us in any way he could. He pointed to a house in the distance, half hidden in the snow-covered hills and said that that was where he lived and that we must come to him for anything we needed.

Just the sight of this sturdy Norwegian with his jolly face and kind manner gave us new confidence; we happily promised to remember his kind offer. One of the skiers then recognised me, and said she had just left Bergen where she had seen our landlady,

'The boy led the way'.

and she had promised us that she would take care of all our belongings. After these cheering encounters we started on the last short mile, and soon the car stopped by the roadside. Several hundred yards away there were a few little tourist shacks, but the house which we were seeking could not be seen from the road. We shouldered all our packages, the children and one of the youths all staggering in the snow under large parcels. The boy led the way in the deep virgin snow and at last we reached our shack.

It was delightful to walk into a little house again. The oil lamp which hung over the dining table was soon lighted and we saw with pleasure that everything was prepared for us.

Fresh curtains were at the small windows, blankets on the beds, and the whole hut was so clean and welcoming. There was a kitchen and large living room downstairs, and three small loft-like rooms above. The living room had a large bed covered by a handwoven rug, a good stove, many chairs and cushions, and photographs and pictures on the walls. The Stoddarts took this room and we moved our family upstairs.

We soon had a cold meal ready and afterwards lost no time in getting to bed. Janet slept in a camp bed in our room and Simon had a small room by the tiny landing. When we finally blew out our candles George and I thought with thankfulness of all the kindness we had met with that day, and so hidden away and safe did we feel that we slept that night without fear.

Chapter Eight

NEXT MORNING, SIMON, ALWAYS AN EARLY RISER, WAS UP early, and managed to light the kitchen stove. We heard him bringing in wood from the well-stocked wood pile in the shed outside and there was later considerable clanking of fire-irons and pans. He brought us all, in turn, hot water for washing, and we were all soon out of bed and hungry for breakfast. This was Simon's self-appointed task the whole time we spent there, and during the day he would chop wood with the men.

Now we dressed for the first time in the clothes we had bought. We all had thick boots and double socks and, with the exception of Janet for whom I'd not been able to get them, we all had trousers. (She had been prepared to wear boy's trousers but was frowned upon!) Still I had bought her thick knickers and a jersey, a woollen cap and a fine yellow anorak, so she was cosy enough, except for very cold legs in the snow.

When George had left Bergen he had actually no collar on his shirt as he had only had time to throw a silk scarf around his neck. Now his golden beard had begun to grow, and as he had no razor he decided to let it grow rather than borrow Stoddart's.

The fire was going well and Simon slipped down the steps again to start cooking us 'a jolly good breakfast' of eggs and bacon. However here a hitch occurred and as we dressed upstairs we heard a polite argument below. Soon Simon appeared upstairs again, looking his sulkiest.

'It's all off', he said. 'You're going to have boiled potatoes instead.' His expression was quite tragic, for he always loved wielding a frying pan and cooked a better breakfast than any of us, and ate enormous amounts always.

'Mrs. Stoddart says we must save the eggs and bacon' he told us mournfully. 'She insists on boiled potatoes for breakfast, which I think is mad.' We shook with silent laughter and implored Simon to be good and take whatever was coming.

George went downstairs and found the atmosphere a bit strained while the Stoddarts argued as to what we should eat. Mrs. Stoddart was chagrined that her suggestion was taken so badly by the hungry men, and the potatoes on the stove were set aside for lunch.

We ate boiled eggs as a compromise. The incident was soon forgotten, but it shook me rather to see such high feelings over such a trivial matter. From now on the Russian temperament was to be our greatest trial, and if I do not mention our friend for days at a time it is because for one imagined offence or another she was not speaking to any of us.

But this morning we were soon all busy tidying up the house and washing dishes. Mrs. Stoddart said she would do the cooking, so the rest of us took over other jobs to be done. For several days, until she gave up all tasks in the hut, she did our cooking which consisted almost entirely of a nourishing boiled stew. Everything went into the pot and, though it was good, our insides rather rebelled after a while and we longed for something to chew. It was comic how when often we would stand still in sudden fright, straining to identify suspicious sounds we fancied we heard, our insides would growl fiercely in the silence, in chorus and solo, and the tension would be relieved by our inevitable laughter.

We had promised the good friend who had lent us our hideout, that we would be as inconspicuous as possible, and we only went out of doors singly and talked always in low voices. The sun was bright and warm and the deep snow around us untrodden except for the track we had made when we arrived last night.

The only sound was the noise of the heavy German bombers. We would hear their distinctive throbbing engines in the distance, and soon the heavy plane would pass low over us. We wondered where they were going and what was the next move they were planning. We felt we must have news, so George and I, feeling we looked the most like Norwegians, decided this first morning to go and find out what we could.

We took with us a red milk-pail which we found in the house and started off to explore. As we retraced our tracks in the deep snow, George leading the way, we did not speak, and with great apprehension we descended to the main road. All was quiet, frighteningly quiet, and not a soul in sight. Still without a whisper we climbed off the road and made for a large hut; George seeming to know by instinct that here we could get small provisions.

It proved to be a tiny hotel, but no-one was about as we pushed open the door and made our way to a small counter. George rapped on the wood with the milk pail and presently a small boy appeared. We asked for milk and bought some cigarettes and George casually asked for news. The boy seemed as ignorant as we, but told us that no supplies were coming through and there was no bread. We bought our milk and said we would come again the next morning for more, and turned homeward again. We passed several men and girls but no one spoke, so still in silence we reached our hut again.

No news and there was nothing to do but wait and plan. We had acquired a map of the country and now began the many hours we were to spend poring over it, with mounting anxiety. Should we stay where we were or should we move higher into the mountains? Always the hope that the British would land near us soon kept us resolved to stay hidden as we were a little longer. There seemed no likelihood of the Germans pushing on at once, and only the ever-present bomber overhead reminded us of the grim fact that we were in danger. If this had been a peaceful holiday, how we could have revelled in our surroundings; the snowy slopes were perfect for skiing, and the air so invigorating that it was hard to remain quietly indoors.

The same evening about five o'clock George decided to try to find Herr O—, the man who had pointed out his house and offered to help us. George was gone for over an hour and we watched anxiously for his return. Simon could not resist going out in the dusk to meet him; then we saw him struggling back up the track. I watched them from the door clap each other on the back without a word and beam at each other. There was a grand feeling between them. The Stoddarts stopped their endless card game to hear the news. George had found the house and our new friend had welcomed him in and shown a great concern for us and desire to help. They had listened to the wireless and though there was no good news for us, still we felt that we were in touch with the world again. Regularly every night afterwards George went over to the house and listened in and, when the radio broke down, Herr O— took him to another family he trusted, and so we got news every day.

On the third day we were all playing rummy, with the exception of Mrs. Stoddart who was very depressed and had rather taken to her bed, when we were startled by a knock at the door. We had heard no sound and now our hearts beat quickly with fright. George opened the door and to our relief we saw our landlady and a young girl standing there. They had come on skis through the woods above us, and so we had not seen or heard them approach. They were very hot and out of breath, and seemed considerably alarmed.

'Are you all right?' were their first words as they stamped the snow off their boots and came inside. That day we were feeling very cheerful and optimistic and our friend marvelled to find us in such good spirits; they, on the contrary, were very frightened and with good reason. They had been listening daily to the broadcasts from Oslo, where the Germans had taken over, and always these announcements ended with the threat that anyone helping the British would be severely punished. (Within a week or two this punishment became bluntly 'will be shot', but at this time the Germans were anxious to appear friendly.)

Our friends had wondered if we were still in the hut or if we had fled, and with great kindness Fru Sandven had had a sack of provisions dumped in an empty hut some distance away. She offered to leave us a pair of skis so that one of us could follow their tracks and fetch it. As for news, they knew as little as we did. The Germans were still concentrating on Bergen and had as yet made no attempt to come further inland. The young girl's fiance had been called up and had left for his regiment the previous day.

After staying only a few minutes our visitors left on foot, leaving their skis with us. Again we studied our map, and talked and talked of possible routes we could take, but as usual there seemed no place safer than our present one. Yet we had seen how we were endangering our friends and knew we must move soon.

Later that day George decided to retrieve the sack of provisions.

Although he had not skied since we lived in Stockholm, twelve years previously, he was the only one among us who could attempt it. It proved quite an undertaking and his account of it when he returned hot and exhausted, proved it had been more than he had bargained for. He had started off by the road on foot, carrying his skis, having a shrewd idea where this empty hut lay. He had found it without trouble, and the promised sack on the small veranda. It was a large sack, half full, and on the top of all he saw a box labelled 'eggs'. Rather dismayed he had opened it to make sure it really contained eggs, and found about two dozen, neatly packed. He had been in half a mind to leave them knowing his unreliability on skis. But eventually he had succeeded in putting on his skis, shouldering the cumbersome sack, and with two sticks in his free hand had shot off across the snow.

The women had been expert skiers and their tracks showed where they had leapt over small chasms, and dashed with speedy swerving over the slopes in fine fashion. Poor George had been hard put to it to follow their trail and would have rather picked an easier way, but was afraid of losing his direction in the woods. According to him, he had made some wonderful flights, invariably ending up buried in the snow, but always with the sack and precious eggs held aloft. Again and again he had taken terrific falls but never failed to save the eggs. He arrived panting and triumphant and grinning as he laid the sack reverently before us on the floor.

We surrounded him with praise and laughter.

'How *did* you manage it?' we cried.

'You don't know the half of it', George panted, 'there are eggs in there and they are probably all cracked.' We rushed to see, and to our amazement every egg was whole – not a single one even cracked.

'Hah!' said George and beat himself on the chest while we looked at him with something like awe.

That night Simon was to make an omelette for supper, for it was his speciality and we had so many eggs we could afford to revel in them – but no omelette was forthcoming. Simon found he could scarcely break the shells. They were all hard-boiled.

We had been in our hut for four days when, everything looking peaceful as usual, George and Stoddart set off to listen to the news. We had always been afraid that in these expeditions odd Germans

'The motor cycles ridden by German soldiers'.

or spies might be encountered and though George with his fair hair and fluent Norwegian would cause no suspicion, Stoddart looked a typical towny Englishman and could not speak a word of the language; but tonight they both set off with confidence.

They returned sooner than expected, and I, who happened to be in the wood-shed, saw them appear out of the wooded hills above the house. I felt there was something wrong; they looked strained, but they did not say anything. When we asked for news they said there was nothing fresh, and we set about getting supper ready. Later that night when the children were asleep, George told me of the awful fright they had had, and how they had not heard the radio at all.

They had set off for Herr O—'s house and come down onto the main road. The way led along the road for about twenty minutes when they would have to leave it and pick their way over the snow to a house a few hundred yards away. They had been walking for a short time when they heard in the still air the sound of a motor, and soon they turned and saw motor-cycles coming up behind them.

'Keep straight on', George had whispered and they had plodded on, not daring to look behind again and hoping they would not be spoken to. The motor-cycles, ridden by German soldiers, passed them and disappeared into the distance.

Soon they heard the sound of a car, and as they kept on walking they wondered if this was the vanguard of a German advance approaching. The car, laden with German officers, passed, and when it was out of sight George and Stoddart slipped off the road and climbed the high snow bank to get to the woods. They had come back by a roundabout way and our anxiety on hearing this news can be imagined. All night we wondered if the Germans were moving their troops, and whether next morning we would find ourselves in German-occupied territory and our escape cut off.

Chapter Nine

NEXT MORNING WAS AS QUIET AND STILL AS EVER. NOT A sound could we hear as we listened anxiously for the sound of traffic on the road. Encouraged by the silence, and feeling we must know if the Germans had advanced, George and I visited the place where we had bought provisions. Only the young boy was there and as he did not offer any news we bought the last packets of cigarettes and came home again.

We tried to pass the day as best we could. The men chopped wood in the shed. We played cards and Simon experimented with boards tied to his feet as snow shoes.

From the first day in the hut Mrs. Stoddart had begun to write her experiences in an exercise book she had bought, and rather apprehensively we watched her write pages and pages in Russian. George suggest to Stoddart that, though we would all like to keep a diary, it was a dangerous thing to do, and would not be fair to the good people who had helped us so far. The result was that our Russian companion refused to eat or speak with us and continued her writing under our noses. At night her husband would take the book and hide it in the wood-shed.

This evening, after the sight of the Germans the previous day, George went off to visit Herr O— at the usual time to get the radio news. By great good fortune he met there a Norwegian army officer and a naval officer who had been stationed that day in a house nearby. They had a long talk together, and we, left behind in the hut, were worried about him long before we saw his silhouette climbing towards us in the half-light.

We had news and plans at last.

George had learned that this very day other car-loads of Germans had passed along the road, unknown to us, and on reaching the end of the mountain pass had been fired on by Norwegian soldiers. One car which had been disabled was immediately set alight by the Germans, and the other, carrying several wounded men, had raced back along the road to Bergen.

After this attack we felt sure that the Germans would send a stronger force very soon. The younger army officer said he was in touch by telephone with other outposts nearer Bergen, and he would let us know if Germans came along our road that night. The naval officer said that he was in communication with the British Navy and he would try his best to help us.

'This means', said George, 'that we must leave here as soon as it is light tomorrow, and be prepared before we go to bed, in case we must go suddenly in the night.'

George had arranged that if we did not get word during the night, we would leave the hut about 7 am next morning. Our good friend Herr O— would take us in his car to the next town, Norheimsund, and the army would hold the mountain pass open for us until we came.

At once we set about packing our belongings and cleaning and tidying the hut as best we could. One thing George insisted on: he said he would not take the Stoddarts with us if the account she had written was not destroyed before we went. The dangerous pages were torn out of the book by the writer herself and burnt in the stove. Now all our things were packed George and Stoddart shaved, the former sacrificing a lovely curly beard which we had all taken quite a pride in.

We all went to bed fully dressed with our boots handy by our bedsides ready to pull on, and all night I listened against my will for the footsteps which might come to summon us. This truly was one of the most nerve-racking nights we had ever spent. About midnight we heard the sudden boom of distant gunfire at sea, and this sinister, intermittent firing continued until dawn. The children and George slept, but the whole night I lay rigid, my ears foolishly straining to catch the least suspicious sound and the crackling of the snow and creaking trees convinced me time and time again that the next moment I would hear a loud knock on our door.

At five o'clock we were glad to get up and eat a hurried breakfast. We had time to finish tidying the hut and the last packing of our ill-assorted belongings. It was a real problem for us, for we still had only Janet's small school case for four of us. The Stoddarts had bought a rucksack for their things, but we had not been able to get one. There was a shortage of rucksacks at this time, as so many had been sent to Finland. Eventually the famous provision sack took a heavy load for George, and I had my fur coat and other things in a white pillow case.

At seven o'clock we stepped into the snow and closed the door quietly behind us. It was snowing, and still only half light. George led the way, then Simon with a large paper parcel, then Janet with her teddy-bear in a paper bag, its head looking out of the top and a little hat on its head. Next came me, with my pillow case, my anorak soon wet through with the snow, and the Stoddarts took up the rear. Without a sound we descended to the road; not a soul was about, and with a strange feeling of nightmare we spread out in a single file along the road.

After walking about fifteen minutes, a Norwegian officer caught us up, and with a salute to George whom he must have recognised, passed us. Suddenly he looked behind us, and leapt quickly onto the high snow bank, and put his binoculars to his eyes, scanning the distance behind us, and with what fears in our hearts we broke into a jog trot! I saw George look behind over his huge sack, but I looked no further than our companions who were keeping up with us. I did not dare look further for I feared what I might see.

We left the soldier behind and came at last to our meeting-place, where a large lorry gave us a little shelter. Fortunately there was no sign of any other traffic on the road; the soldier must have had a false alarm. In our anxiety to be moving we had arrived early and we now stood and shivered for about half an hour before George went to fetch Herr O—.

We talked with a charming Norwegian officer who had been expecting us, who assured us that the mountain road would be closed after we had passed over it. Soon Herr O— emerged well wrapped up in a leather coat and skiing cap, carrying a spade and a tin of petrol. He was so merry and matter-of-fact that my spirits recovered with a bound and it was with great relief and joy that at

'Suddenly he looked behind us'.

last we climbed into his car and started off. Just to be moving was a release from strain. Every yard of the way added to one's feeling of security and soon Janet and I in front with Herr O— were laughing and as cheerful as he.

For the third time we slid onto the dreaded road, and once more we skidded and stuck in the snow, but our driver was so confident and skilful that I for one did not suffer so much.

'Here comes the nasty bit', Herr O— would laugh. 'Over she goes!' and over she went without mishap. When the car could not move, he leapt out and began shovelling away the snow at a terrific rate. Then into the car again, and,

'Hold tight here! Steady does it and over she goes!' and again we were putting miles behind us.

Herr O— pointed out to us the very spot where the German car had been stopped the day before. He was elated at this and assured us that the valuable pass was already mined and that should the

Germans come along it, it would be sacrificed to keep them back. We learned later this was not to be. Traitors saw to it that the mines were not fired, and the Germans later passed along it with only the inadequately armed Norwegians endeavouring in vain to stop them.

As we left the pass and drove on to the straight flat road to the town we passed a large bus full of armed Norwegian soldiers, which had been waiting for our arrival; on our appearance it started off up the mountains. How sad the young faces of the soldiers looked, almost, I thought, like cattle being shipped to the slaughter-house. Fervently I wished that this would not be true and that these lives would not be sacrificed.

For the second time within a week we entered the town of Norheimsund which lay at the head of the fjord. Down here the snow had gone weeks ago, and there was even a feeling of spring in the air. Everywhere we saw fruit trees and bright grass, and as we came in sight of the fjord, the sun came out to turn the water a deeper blue. Herr O— drove us straight to the Hotel and into the courtyard at the back. We got out, unseen by the townsfolk, and by back stairs were led quickly to a private bedroom. A maid appeared and lit the enamelled stove in the corner, and soon the room began to warm up. We were chilled to the bone and our outer coverings were wet through. We took off what we could and gratefully relaxed after our exciting journey.

Soon our kind friend Fru Sandven, who owned the hotel, came in and congratulated us on our timely escape. She ordered a huge breakfast for us to be brought into our room and went off at once, for she had work to do. She was in the midst of fitting up a part of the hotel as a hospital, and outside in the garden we could see a stack of hastily made wooden beds waiting to be moved inside. At this time everyone fully expected that there would be a fight to hold the pass, and felt confident that the Germans would fail.

Herr O— had left us immediately to seek out a hiding place for us, and as we waited we saw him several times from our window as he hurried here and there about his business. After we had eaten and our clothes were almost dried by the hot stove, I lay down on the sofa for a short rest. The children were in fine spirits and the rest of the party smoked and talked, but I felt completely exhausted and could not stop shivering. Still, this soon passed with no-one

"He emerged carrying a spade in one hand"

but myself the wiser of it, and when Herr O— reappeared we were all eager and ready to be off.

We got into the car again and drove for a very short distance through the small town and out to the outskirts. We could easily have walked, but we attracted no attention in the car with Herr O— at the wheel. We stopped at the back door of a small summer house which looked straight onto the water; Herr O— got out first and talked to the group of women lounging by the door.

A terrific argument began in a dialect we could not follow, and then continued lustily indoors, while we in the car could hear our friend gradually getting the best of it. At last he returned and told us to get out and come inside. With our pathetic bundles we stepped quickly through the group of curious women and were shown into a large dining room. We dropped our packages on the floor and waited for Herr O— to tell us where we were and what we were expected to do.

'You can hide here safely for a day or two', he said. 'I have impressed on these people that they must not talk, and it is still so early that no one knows you are here. They were unwilling at first, because it is a risk for them, and these rooms really belong to a family who have just evacuated themselves further inland. However you must make yourselves as comfortable as you can and I'll send Lieut. K— as soon as I find him.'

It was hard to thank him enough for his wonderful assistance. He passed off our thanks as unnecessary and went off, as cheery as ever, to load his car with provisions and to try to get back to his family. Next day, we saw him in the distance, still in town, still striding energetically from place to place, still unable to get home again.

We explored our quarters and found a tiny kitchen and a room with a single bed. We took it in turns to stretch out and relax and intermittently we played cards and talked of what our next move was likely to be. After an hour or two the door opened and the naval officer whom George had met the night before entered the room with another man. This man, a businessman in Bergen, was, we thought, really brought in to identify George and Stoddart; by good luck George and he remembered each other. After George had a long free discussion with the two men, and they came to the conclusion that we must wait, perhaps an hour or two, until some conveyance could be sent to take us out to the coast. The naval officer looked ready to drop with fatigue. He had not been in bed for three nights, and was unshaven and quite glassy-eyed. But again he dashed off to urgent affairs promising to let us know as soon as he could. We must wait in patience – the most difficult thing to do.

The old lady of the house came in and lit a fire for us, and gave us a huge bowl of oranges which, she explained, were some which had been given them. A few days before, an orange ship, unable to get into the port of Bergen to sell them, had come up the fjord and proceeded to give oranges away to any family who cared to carry them. We were most grateful for our share, and throughout our stay in this district we had as many as we cared to eat. Later we were to see children, who had previously had perhaps one orange for Christmas eating one or two dozens a day!

At about 2 pm a charming little girl and boy arrived at our door with a huge hamper from the hotel. The table was laid and we proceeded to have a marvellous meal: chicken soup, roast lamb and a wonderful cream cake as a desert. We all felt distinctly better for the good food and the afternoon passed peacefully.

George and Stoddart now decided that something must be done about money. Fru Sandven had advanced us so much for our clothes and food, and she now very generously returned to me the jewellery I had left with her a week before. George resolved to try if the banks would lend something, and armed with a paper signed by Stoddart and himself, a promissory note on the British Government, he went off alone to try his luck. He was away for several hours, but came back with a generous amount of kroners in cash. At first he had met with no success, but by great perseverance he had gone from one man to another and eventually assembled a meeting of the governors of the local bank. They were mostly small farmers and businessmen, and they had listened sympathetically to George as he stated his case, finally unanimously deciding to accept the note and advance him the money he asked.

We shall always be grateful to these generous men. It was a fine thing for them to have trusted their money to this unknown Britisher, and yet it was to be typical of the Norwegians' generosity, and their confidence, which they were always ready to give George when he asked it.

As night came on we cooked ourselves a simple meal and waited expectantly for news. It was nearly ten o'clock when a messenger, the son of Fru Sandven, came to tell us that it was unlikely that word would come until next day, and that some of us could sleep at the hotel if we went in by the back way.

The Stoddarts decided to go, but we stayed in case a message should come after all. At the last minute after trying our scanty sleeping accommodation, Simon ran out after them, and also spent a good night in the comfortable Sandven Hotel. George lay on the divan in the dining room, and Janet and I shared the small bed. We took only our boots off, and prepared to have as good a night as we could.

Next morning we waited eagerly for our friends to come back, so we could go and have a bath and breakfast. Simon appeared well fed and clean, and at nine o'clock we were unable to restrain ourselves any longer and walked over to the hotel. Our friends were still eating breakfast after a luxurious night, and after a short time we too were appreciating good coffee and eggs. George had a quick bath, but Janet and I had to go without in case we were taking too long and were being waited for at our hiding place. We asked for our bill, and had great satisfaction in paying Fru Sandven everything we owed her with our newly borrowed money.

Several times that day we made careful visits into the town, and walked by the fjord. George bought a few things we needed – an extra blouse for me, more stockings and a razor and a pair of scissors. He came back at lunchtime with meat and potatoes which I cooked in the little kitchen, and at tea-time we were able to brew tea and eat biscuits. The day passed slowly and every moment we expected to be called away. A message came that we would probably leave about 8 pm, so we packed up everything and waited. At ten o'clock we were still waiting.

The townspeople had been told to black out their windows, and the electricity was turned off at dusk so that we only had a single candle to light our room. After Janet had exhausted all games of patience and card-houses, she had the bright idea of collecting several boxes of matches and emptying them onto the table. For hours we played spillikins with them, Janet always winning because her hand was the steadiest.

About midnight we heard a knock at the door, and Fru Sandven's son came in to say that we would not be leaving until the next morning. This would probably be about 7 am, so we must be ready early. Once more we prepared to spend the night as comfortably as we could. The two Stoddarts took the divan, and as he was very thin and she was short and plump, they managed to squash up together. George lay down on the bare floor with a coat for a pillow, while Simon and Janet slept in the bed. I lay across the bottom amongst their feet, and a more uncomfortable position could hardly be imagined. We did not dare even to take our boots off, for fear we should have to leave in a rush – and in the dark my boots and Janet's would take a long time to put on.

I lay for hours wide awake while my feet tickled and jumped, and the children's boots occasionally jabbed me in the face or ribs as they slept. After an hour or two, the Stoddarts, who also must have found sleep impossible, got up and sat round the candle and smoked cigarettes. The 'temperament' began to show itself again and George's character was pulled to shreds. The unlucky husband loyally said nothing, but in a piercing whisper we heard,

'What danger has this Villiers got us into now? It is probably all a plot and we are trapped. We'll never get away from here and it is all his doing. He is a fool and talks too much. Look how he talks to all these people who are not to be trusted. He takes too much on himself and is a complete fool. We'll never get out of this – what a mad fool.'

How different from the mild approval that had greeted his return with the money a few hours before! But this was to be our experience of this woman throughout the weeks we spent together, and as it distressed me more than the danger we were in I shall try not to mention her continual bitter recriminations and moods again; but that night the terrible tirade went on and on, while George blissfully snored at their feet on the floor.

Janet and Simon woke up as the voice was raised higher and higher and were rather alarmed.

'How can she say such things?' quavered Janet, her face showing a trace of fright for the first time. I tried to reassure them, and myself when I whispered,

'Daddy knows what he is doing, you may be sure. He would not be sleeping so soundly if he thought there was any danger. Tomorrow we'll be away to meet a British ship, and we'll look back and laugh at the funny night we have spent.'

Eventually the children dropped off to sleep again and in the early hours, when the voice at last was quiet, I too slept.

We were all up early, and had our bundles packed in good time. From the window, we watched the road anxiously. Just after 7 am a lorry drew up before the house, and Fru Sandven's son jumped down from the driver's seat and ran to our door. We picked up our baggage and quietly followed him to the car. Two of us sat in the front with the driver and the others jumped up behind and sat on the floor. We drove off along the winding road, through lovely fields and orchards, and after an hour we reached another inlet of the fjord.

The Norwegian Navel Patrol boat D/S Haus, commanded by Captain Bugge

With what delight we saw a Norwegian boat waiting for us by the shore! Once more I thanked so inadequately the good boy who had brought us here. He went off to fight the same day. We quickly boarded the ship where our naval friend was waiting to welcome us. He took us straight to a comfortable cabin where a fine breakfast was already laid for us. Immediately the boat, flying the Norwegian flag, moved off into the deep water of the fjord and with gathering speed we set off in the direction of the coast; as we fondly believed, to get in touch with the British Navy.

Chapter Ten

After our much needed breakfast it was pleasant to lean over the rails and watch the changing scene as we went up the fjord. For the most part sheer cliffs dropped to the water's edge, but often here and there we would come upon a little house with a green patch of grass in front and a tiny boat-house. At first we saw few humans about these remote farms, but as the morning warmed up a few solitary figures would stop their work to watch our fine boat go by. We wondered a little if the odd aeroplanes we saw flying high above us had any interest in our passage, but we felt we were in good hands and soon relaxed to bask in the sun for the first time for many days. The children were soon chatting with the friendly crew, one of whom gave Janet a little bag of sweets which was to last her many weeks. George went off with the Lieutenant and they had long discussions together about their plans.

After about five hours had passed we began to look out for the place we were to land and soon we saw a tiny village ahead with a fair-sized landing stage. Some minutes before we drew up alongside, the women and children of our party were gathered into the cabin and told not to show themselves. For perhaps half an hour we laid low, catching glimpses through the curtains of the interested crowd on the jetty and listening to their animated talk. Then we were told we could come out on deck where again we waited some time.

Simon spied a school friend of his in the crowd and they waved to each other and shouted remarks back and forth. Only a few yards away was another ship like ours. It was moored close in to the land beside some trees, and was heavily camouflaged with branches and greenery. This little village of Eslervik had been chosen by the Norwegian Navy as one of its headquarters and at this time they believed that they were in direct touch with the British by radio.

Our lieutenant had left us and gone to the village to report to his superior officers and when he came back in the transport he had arranged for us we were allowed to disembark. We all climbed into the waiting lorry and were driven through the tiny village and then perhaps for a mile and a half further on. Here the road turned abruptly at right angles and we stopped at the gate of a large white house. We were led into the garden, and our guide went inside to arrange beds for us; we sat about in the sun and waited. Soon another naval officer, looking as if he had just wakened up and still fastening on his uniform coat, came and shook hands with us. We learned he had been up for the last forty-eight hours without sleep, and had just been snatching a well-earned rest when we came. He assured us that rooms were being prepared for us, and without more ado he took George and Mr. Stoddart off with him in his car.

Mrs. Stoddart, the children and I still waited in the garden. We were beginning to feel sleepy now and several times I caught myself dozing off on my hard bench. To keep ourselves awake we began to walk about and our Russian, who had been in a huff for a long time, went and sat far away from us. But soon we heard her imitating the little white cock that strutted among the hens and she did it so well that the poor bird was driven quite frantic and made us all laugh with its efforts to outdo her crows. We were pleased to be friends again and soon we were all chatting happily together.

At last we were invited into the house and with relief we saw the comfortable rooms we had been given. The Stoddarts had a fine large room, and our family had one room with three beds in it and another attic with a communicating door with another small bed. We looked at these with great approval and gaily I promised that tonight Janet and I should sleep in our nightgowns, which we had never yet worn. George and Mr. Stoddart did not return to the house until nearly four o'clock when we had already had lunch, rested, and explored our surroundings.

This house, which was to prove such a landmark in our

VILLIERS.

STODDART.

FOTOGRAF RØVDE - ROSENDAL

Hr. Kapt Hauge

Adr. Uskedal

No

Fotografi 4 passfoto — 5.–

Postkørt

Fremkaldt

Kopiert

Førstørrelser Rosendal 20/4-40

In Norwegian Naval uniform for identity papers, April 1940.
Photos found in Rosendal by Gunnar Strandenes in 1998

journeyings, was a typical old Norwegian farm house, now used as a guest house. Its huge lofty rooms were papered with the most amazing old wallpaper, known to be over a hundred years old, and much of its decoration and furniture must have been in the house since it was built. The kitchen had the largest and most beautiful array of copper pans that I had ever seen, and everywhere was shining cleanliness. As Janet remarked, seeing the dazzling white paint everywhere,

'Everything is white; even the hens and chickens match.'

The day passed in a frenzy of activity. It was arranged that a telephone would be installed in the house immediately and it was duly fixed up to connect us with the naval headquarters down the road. George had endless talks with the officers there, and for safety's sake it was decided that both the Englishmen should be given commissions in the Norwegian navy. Everybody realised that should they be captured without uniform they could be instantly shot as spies, and so the sooner they were made officers the better. So George and Stoddart made a lengthy expedition by car to another village and there, in borrowed caps and jackets, had their photographs taken for their official papers. They were also measured there and then for their uniforms, which were to be ready the following day. Finally being utterly convinced by these keen Norwegians that they were actually in touch with British headquarters by telephone, they resolved to send a message asking for help.

The message was telephoned by George himself that night, giving full directions for a successful entrance up the fjord to our position, with passwords and other details, and he gave his full name and the ranks of himself and Stoddart as proof of their good faith and genuineness. With this accomplished we were all in fine spirits that night, when after a good dinner we went happily to bed. George felt he saw success in sight, and such was our confidence that we took off all our clothes to sleep.

Mercifully we did not know what treachery was afoot and what disaster lay ahead of us. Many hours later, when it was too late, we learned that the English voice which had taken George's message belonged to a German, and that the telephone station was in Quisling hands. Our message was passed on to German naval forces, and as we slept peacefully the Germans followed our directions and closed upon our village.

Chapter Eleven

DURING THE NIGHT I WOKE TO HEAR THE DISTANT SHRILLING of the newly installed telephone. Its urgent voice had me half awake impatient for its clamour to be silenced. No one seemed to be stirring in the sleeping house to answer it, and the insistent ringing went on. Tonight at least I had no cause to be straining my ears in dread, and I tried to sleep again. Drowsily I imagined someone on his way to answer it. A slippered old man probably, I could see him still pulling on his coat, muttering to himself in the dark passage. Now at last his hand would be stretching to lift off the receiver. But no, the ringing still continued unanswered. Eventually half-dreaming of other servants hurrying to answer it, I dropped off to sleep again. So the warning went unheeded.

It could not have been long after when the terrific 'zoomp' of a near explosion shook the house. The heavy crashes were repeated again and again while bright flashes lit up the dark window. Then in the startling silence that followed we heard the angry sound of aeroplanes flying low. Hurriedly I pulled on my trousers over my nightdress, thrust my arms into a jersey and pulled on my boots. George ran to get Simon up while I hastily flung some clothes on Janet. A minute or two later we descended the stairs, to meet most of the other guests in the hall. The sounds had come from the direction of the little village where we had landed yesterday, but now there was an ominous silence.

After a minute or two we opened the door and went out into the garden. It was not yet dawn and all was quiet. There were perhaps a dozen people there, all inwardly alarmed and puzzled for no-one could imagine what had happened; but no-one talked much. After a short time and still no further sounds, we turned to go to our rooms again. Once more we tucked up the children and lay down half-dressed on our beds, and as we listened to the stillness it was hard to believe that we had really heard that terrifying din. We persuaded ourselves and the children that perhaps a mine had exploded in the fjord. We would hear all about it in the morning.

'Good night again', we called to each other, now almost amused by our scare.

We had just settled down to sleep again when another shattering explosion blasted us wide awake. But this time the firing went on. We heard the unmistakable thump of bombs and the drone of aeroplanes, and through it all the sharp crack of hand grenades and rifles. In urgent haste we got the children up again. Our clothes were more difficult to find this time. Our boots were mislaid and it was almost impossible to get our feet into them, so frantic were we. (Later that night I was to discover Janet wearing one of my boots and I one of hers. There was two sizes difference, but I never noticed it.) We snatched up blankets and once again hurried down the stairs. People had collected in the tiny hall, listening to the bombing with anxious faces. After a minute or two the volume of sound increased and the rattle of machine guns drowned the intermittent rifles.

With one accord, we descended into the cellar and stood about with blankets wrapped round us. Suddenly George remembered that the jacket of a naval officer, which had been lent him, had been left in our room, and without hesitation one of the visitors, a civilian, ran back up the stairs, and helped hide it in the cellar. It was now about 4.30 am, a favourite hour for a German attack. We talked hopefully with the others, and listened to the now continuous firing, trying to believe that it was lessening or going further away – but it was without a doubt coming nearer to us.

The next moment, as we stood there, the crack of rifles sounded in the garden, and we heard the thud of bullets on the wall. A stray bullet came through the little window and rattled against a small dried-up tree which stood on the floor. As we looked at it still swaying from the impact, another bullet whistled past Simon's head. Seeing him clap his hand to his head in surprise we realised

The cellar in Kapteinsgården, Uskedal.

that we would be safer sitting down, so we quickly laid blankets against the outside wall and, with the children between us, sat with our backs to it – only half the cellar walls were above ground, the window being at ground level. We wrapped the children in the remaining blankets, while the others sat on the stairs and in other corners out of the line of fire.

For the next two or three hours we kept these positions, silent and frightened, while I prayed inwardly and urged the children to pray too. They were so good and brave; I felt their prayers would count more than ours. The firing of machine guns was now all around us and we grew accustomed to the thudding of bullets on the wall at our backs.

It was now obvious that we were in the centre of a fight which was going on round the house, and that Norwegians and Germans must have met at the crossroads. One man with a rifle – a Norwegian we thought – took up a position lying in the hollow by our window and for hours we listened to him just over our heads, until he was shot and died groaning and gurgling horribly. Gradually we felt the press of more men around us. We heard German voices giving commands, shouting wildly and then a scream or two in the confusion when someone was wounded. They were upon us. We felt now there was no more escape.

Janet was holding one of George's hands, Simon the other. We looked at each other over their heads, pale and numbed.

'This is the end, George', I whispered in a matter of fact voice, though in anguish. 'We can never get out of this.'

'Yes, I'm afraid it looks like it', George assented, just as unemotional, just as anguished, and he began to turn out his pockets. He gave me his note-case with all the money we had. He would not need any. Then he ate a little paper that had a note or two on it. We had our rough bundles there beside us. I desperately looked over the few possessions he might be allowed to take with him. A pair of socks, the clothes he had worn when he left Bergen.

I was worried too that I had not dressed properly. I still had my nightdress underneath though thankfully I knew the children were properly clothed. At that moment the thought of being led through the streets half-clothed, and the thought of George's poor wardrobe, worried me more than the noise so close to us. Then I forgot it; the clash was all around us.

'Pray darlings, don't stop for a moment', I whispered to the poor children. We were all praying in our hearts, I think; that was why we all looked so remote, so calm. Only a miracle could save us, so we prayed for that.

'Hände hoch!' we heard a German shout, and again ' Hande hoch!' and the firing gradually died away. The ensuing silence was terrifying. We heard quite plainly the footsteps to the door. Then came a loud banging.

'Open the door! Open the door!' shouted a voice in German, and that terrible banging echoing through the listening house.

Our hostess, who had been sitting on the stairs, got up and went out. In amazement we heard her answering the German in his own language. We strained our ears to hear, our hearts so full of dread that one scarcely felt like a living person. Suddenly as we listened, the firing broke out again. There was more rush and clamour outside and the German went away. Then our hostess came into the cellar again.

She had bravely told him that there were only women and refugees in the cellar. The surprise of hearing her speak German must have convinced him, and then the renewed attack had prevented his searching the house there and then. We were a little relieved, but felt it was only a temporary reprieve. Meanwhile the fight began again in earnest, and for interminable hours we listened to the shooting and the shouts around us. We had gone into the cellar at about 4.30 am; at eight o'clock we roused ourselves to whisper that at last it seemed the fight was over. A few intermittent shots would still ring out, but the press around us had gone. Another half hour and it was so quiet that we decided to come into the daylight again.

Cautiously we emerged into the hall. The house was empty, but scarred by numberless bullets. The windows were broken. The lovely wallpaper damaged and plaster from walls and ceilings lay over everything. I had left so many useful things in our bedroom and now that things looked safe, I left the family in the hall and dashed up the stairs three at a time. I could still hear a not-so-distant shot, so for safety's sake I entered our room crouching low on my heels. I reached up with my hand and gathered a few odd things from a table, picked up another jersey, a raincoat, and rejoined the people downstairs.

The good housewife and her two maids had begun to make coffee, and to cut bread and cheese. With shaky hands and dry mouths we ate and drank a little. George found a bottle of whisky he had been given the night before by one of the officers. A lot of spirits had been gratefully collected from a German boat they had captured recently, so now all the men had a welcome tot.

What were we to do now, and what had been the result of the fight? No news by telephone and all the neighbours were still in their homes.

'Let us just walk out as we did in Bergen', I urged. 'If we stay we will certainly be caught. At least let us make a dash for it.' Our friends were reluctant to move.

'Where would we go?'

There were a thousand reasons against it and only my burning

'They drove slowly past us'.

impulse to be up and doing. George and I decided to visit a house across the road; at least they could tell us where the road over the mountains would lead us, and what lay in the other direction. They might know where the Germans were now.

We walked out into the fresh morning. An old woman crept along the road, the only living thing in sight. Then, suddenly, as we stood there hesitating in the garden, we heard the sound of a motor, and the next moment a lorry, bearing a gun and manned by six Germans standing to attention beside it, appeared at the cross-roads. I expected it to stop at our gate, for I thought they must be going to put the gun in the garden.

But they drove slowly past us and out of sight. As soon as they had gone George and I crossed the road, and coming to a little wooden house we knocked on the door. A large family was having breakfast, and I noticed one of the maids who had been in the cellar with us amongst them. They were all rather subdued and not at all interested in us. George asked one man about the roads. We had small children, he explained, and wanted to get them to a safe and peaceful spot. Did he know of any tourist hut in the hills? Any little hotel in the valley? The man could not suggest anything to help, but said that the road to the hills led over high mountains to a fjord on the other side. We left still undecided what to do.

Another discussion with our companions and at last we were all agreed that we should walk out and take a chance. We slipped once more up to our room, and hurriedly collected what we could. Then George shouldered his heavy sack, I my bundle with odd shoes and my fur coat inside, Simon took the little attaché case and a briefcase George had been given the previous day, and Janet cherished the teddy-bear. Then with the Stoddarts following we walked out of the garden and turned left to the hilly road before us.

As we walked along on rather trembling legs, we had a clear view for several hundred yards in the direction of the village. At a point a few hundred yards away the Germans had set a guard, and as we walked we felt them scanning us through their binoculars.

'They are watching us', whispered George, who had had the courage to turn and look at them. 'Walk on and keep your eyes in front.' Janet was told to hold her teddy-bear between us and the Germans which she did, shielding her. Her father said,

'Even a German wouldn't shoot a teddy-bear.'

For some time we felt apprehensive and expected them to stop us. But a hundred yards, then another and another, behind us, and no challenge. Relief began to dawn on us. With our two quite Norwegian-looking children, we must have looked like any other innocent family, moving to a quieter spot after a terrifying night. The Germans were looking for two naval officers, not a party of women and children. Time and time again we were sure it was the presence of the children that saved us.

Now we trudged further and further on, until at last we felt that the small hills hid us from the view of the watch-post. Gradually the road got more stony and wild, and soon we felt that we dare rest a few minutes. Some distance away on our left was a small farmhouse; George set off to see if he could find anyone to direct us. He met a young fellow and after a short talk he rejoined us with the news that the man had gone to fetch his small lorry and that he would give us a lift until the road gave out at the foot of the mountains.

Not long after, as good as his word, our new-found friend drew up beside us in a lorry with a canvas roof, and gratefully we scrambled into it. Two other young men sat with the driver. They were also anxious to get away from the village, now in German hands, and so bumping and lurching along we went deeper and deeper into the wild country. After over an hour of this, we stopped at a tiny house, where our driver commandeered a tall man and a little boy to help us carry our baggage. They would walk with us further on to the next house, which we could see far in the distance at the beginning of the snow line.

Then with our grateful thanks and a small tip, he turned his lorry around and headed for his farm. We had dropped the other two young men somewhere along the way, so now we started off alone with our new guides. It was fine to be walking in the sun again. It was a long pull to our next stopping-place, but we felt such relief and gratitude for our escape that we scarcely noticed it.

When we reached the house our helpers left us to tell the people we were there, while we rested on huge boulders and viewed with delight the sparkling snow ahead of us. The farm people brought us milk, and would have given us food, but none of us were hungry. They told us that many Norwegian soldiers had already passed over the mountains. Some were just ahead of us and could still be seen like flies crawling up the mountainside. Best news of all was that our friend Captain Hauge who had been in command of the base, and whom George had met the day before, had arrived early that morning riding a little horse and had successfully escaped over the mountain.

We thanked them all and picking up our loads started off towards the snow. Now at this height we were still in sight of the village, so we felt that we must climb the mountain as quickly as possible to reach the shelter on the other side. As we rested a moment before descending into a little snow-covered valley before us, we saw another group of black figures not so far ahead of us, laboriously climbing the path we must take. Not knowing the path, we hoped that they would wait for us, and George took handkerchiefs and for some time tried to attract their attention, signalling 'BRITISH' to reassure them. But, after stopping for a short time, they continued their climb; and so we started off in their tracks.

Now we understood why the small figures moved so slowly. The snow was soft and every step was an effort. As we got higher and higher up, the snow was deeper and softer, and soon we were counting every step and resting frequently. But always we felt that we could still be seen by the Germans in the village, and so we pressed on. Looking back we saw five or six black figures arriving at the farm we had just left, then setting off in our track. They carried rifles. We *hoped* that they were Norwegians, and as they had not fired on us, we rightly supposed them to be more soldiers escaping.

We climbed up one hill, only to see another ahead of us, and each hour the going was more difficult. We all showed signs of distress. I had put on my fur coat so as to have less to carry and at least one hand free to fall on, and to help Janet up from time to time. Simon struggled on ahead. George was bowed down with the weight of the sack, and was tempted many times to throw away his overcoat. Sometimes when he fell again and again in the snow I wondered if he would get up again. I remembered the rheumatic fever he had had after rowing at Cambridge and which had done something to his heart, and worried about his white face. Mine on the contrary must have been nearer to purple, for the heat from the sun and our struggles was overpowering. Our companions too felt that the pace was almost too much for them, and as we neared the summit we rested more and more frequently, until a dozen yards at a time was all we could manage. To our pride the children kept up with us with never a grumble or complaint.

After about three hours we found the path ahead of us turned to the left and skirted round the side of the mountain. Another half hour of easy going and at last we began to drop down to the snowless slopes on the other side. We clambered for a long time over large rocks, through pools and over soaking slippery

Signalling 'BRITISH'.

vegetation, and then at last we came out to see thick wooded slopes stretching below us to the fjord. At this moment the group of soldiers that had been following us caught us up, and with them we scrambled and slid into the shelter of the trees.

Here with a party of five or six soldiers we called a halt and gratefully rested and ate, while we waited for our two companions the Stoddarts to catch up with us.

Chapter Twelve

NOW AS WE SAT AND TALKED WITH THE SOLDIERS WHO HAD followed us, we learned a little of what had happened that night. To call them soldiers is rather an exaggeration for only one had anything like a complete uniform. Some had official caps, some uniform jackets, most of them had only an armlet to distinguish them. We examined their rifles and found most were 1890 pattern, and their cartridges were carried loose in leather pouches. One jolly fellow showed us a handful of them, all he had. 'Stick close to me', he said, 'I'm well armed.'

When we remembered the Germans we had seen, with their helmets, pistols, cartridge belts and new weapons, we were overwhelmed at their pluck and audacity. For although the Norwegians had been forced to flee, they had inflicted some losses on the German landing party without a casualty amongst themselves. That first crash we had heard had been a bomb dropped on the poorly camouflaged gun-boat by the quay. Later a landing party had appeared and as they got ashore the Norwegians had fired their gun right into them. The terrific crash which had awakened us the second time had been the first and only shot fired from this gun, for at the same time it had exploded and had thereafter been useless.

As for the rest of the fighting we knew as much as they. After the fight around our house the Norwegians had retreated into the hills leaving the Germans in possession of the village. No doubt they had searched it very thoroughly for us, after we had left.

While they shared some of our chocolate and rested, we could see by their strained white faces that these men had had a desperate time, yet they all had to laugh at the nervousness of the Germans. That one and only shot from their gun had completely wiped out the first landing party and the young Germans who followed after had, according to the soldiers, been too distraught to aim straight with their fine tommy-guns! That was the reason, they said, that so many of them had got away.

After a short time our companions joined us and after they had rested, and because they were beginning to feel chilled, we began again our slippery descent among the trees and rocks.

Sometimes we could not stop ourselves and would go flying headlong, to end up clutching a tree as a brake. Once Simon crashed and skidded past us, landing on his back half out of sight. He picked himself up, before we caught up with him, and we saw him open the briefcase to reassure himself about its contents. To our amazement we saw he had two bottles of whisky, one half-full, tenderly wrapped in a few woollens. We had never thought of it, but he had rescued them and dragged them over the mountain.

'I thought they might be useful', said Simon when we had stopped laughing. They were a very welcome sight too, though we promised ourselves that we would keep them for emergencies.

We continued our slippery progress, and descended rapidly, mostly on our backs. My fur coat was soon covered with mud, but stood the ordeal well. We were just emerging out of the trees when we heard two aeroplanes above us. We froze at once, and with the soldiers around us looked up through the trees at them. Slowly they went over us and passed down the fjord, and we resumed our scramble. At last we came out into the open and saw the still waters of the fjord stretching before us. We could just see two small row-boats at the water's edge, with a group of soldiers waiting beside them.

When our party came up to them, the soldiers with us took places in one of the boats, and when they were all seated with their rifles pointing skywards we helped push the laden boat into the fjord. A few soldiers were left, and we with them climbed into the other boat. Two stalwart boys in jerseys pulled at the oars and slowly we followed the first boat over to the other bank of the fjord.

We had a scare a few minutes later when we were half way across; another aeroplane suddenly appeared and passed quite low directly over us. We felt that the armed soldiers must be easily seen and did not feel too safe in their midst. The men stopped rowing, considering whether to row us back to the nearer shore we had just left, but to our relief the aeroplane passed slowly on its way. We gave our remaining cigarettes to our soldier friends and, not expecting to see them again, wished them goodbye and good luck. Arrived on the other shore, we stepped out and blindly followed behind the men. We walked up a steep path and came into a farmyard. There we all had a drink of water from the pump in the deserted kitchen.

George, as usual, scouted about on his own, and in a nearby lane he encountered Captain Olstrop whom he had met the day before in the village. He was waiting with about twenty of his men who had all straggled in twos and threes to this meeting place. All morning they had been arriving and he had been sending them on to the next village in lorries. This was the last load and they were just waiting for another small party who could be seen coming down the mountain as we had done. He promised to help us on our journey, and when the last men arrived we were packed into the lorry among them. We sat on the front row of benches which had been placed there, and Simon, preferring it, sat on the floor at the back dangling his legs over the edge with the friendly soldiers on each side of him.

We were very tightly packed, but as we sped along the road it was so draughty that we were grateful for the warm bodies around us, and glad to shelter our heads in our hoods. We drove for some miles in this fashion, through the deserted wintry hills, until we came at last to a small village. We drew up in the tiny main street, and after a long wait, we got down to stretch and to try and warm our stiff legs. Soon however we were invited into a house nearby, and taken upstairs to a warm room.

We washed and tidied ourselves a little and from the window watched the practically deserted street. The soldiers had been taken to another place for refreshment, and we gladly heard the preparations for our meal going on in the background.

George, who had been dashing here and there in the village, now returned in time to do justice to the waffles and coffee which appeared at last. The waffles were rather heavy, and we soon felt delightfully full. We paid for the meal, and then prepared to wait for a motor launch which George said would take us across another arm of the fjord. Captain H— was busy getting his men away first, and when they had all gone our party would travel with him in the last boat-load.

I remember this interminable afternoon, chiefly by the sound of a gramophone in the room overhead, playing ' Minuet Capricchio' over and over again. A gay little tune, the children and I had often capered madly to it when it came over the radio in Bergen. When the music ended we could hear a muffled wireless, just too indistinct for the words to be heard. An old woman brought her little granddaughter to see the strange visitors. Janet, who loved nothing better than to play with tiny children, amused her for hours, until she became too attached to our teddy-bear. Janet used to pretend to make him talk, and could use him quite effectively like a ventriloquist uses his doll, making his arms and head work in a very endearing manner. Today she was so convincing that in the end she had to remove the teddy diplomatically and pack him among our luggage.

At last, about six o'clock, we were told to move, and we quickly carried our bundles across the road to a motor-boat, flying the Norwegian flag, which was waiting at the jetty nearby. The forepart was crowded with soldiers, but we had seats in the tiny cabin aft, where Captain Ulstrup joined us.

It was beginning to get dark when we eventually moved off up the fjord. The Captain had a good map with him and the men studied it together as we gathered speed. It was a curious journey for we felt safe and yet unsafe, with the Norwegian flag above us, and the monotonous 'honky-tonk' of the engine echoing over the still, dark waters.

Captain Ulstrup had been so busy looking after his men that he had had no time to feed himself. He was ravenous, and we watched him with amazement open a large tin of meatballs and eat the entire contents there and then. It was while Janet was showing him the flags on the pocket of her sailor dress she was wearing that we suddenly noticed that she and I were wearing each other's boots. It seemed incredible that we had come so many difficult miles and not noticed them. We changed and I suppose one of my numbed feet felt better for it.

We listened to the chatter and singing of the men in the other cabin. Once the Captain had shut them up we all dozed a little. Then after perhaps an hour and a half we realised that we were approaching our destination. High cliffs towered on each side of us, and a tiny village ahead seemed wedged between two tall mountains. We got out, and crossing a little bridge, saw two motor buses waiting to take us further on.

It was cold now. Like the waiting soldiers we visited the tiny village shop, and bought several packets of Sunmaid raisins. The men bought oranges, for they were practically given away, and amid the homely smell of orange peel we waited for the next move on our journey.

Now for the first time I heard that we were going to Odda for the night, but it did not mean much to me until I learned it was the headquarters of the Norwegian Navy. Captain Ulstrup now mustered his men, and they fell into line and stood at attention to hear him speak. I could not follow all of the speech he made to

'Captain Ulstrup mustered his men'.

them, only that they had done well and that they would have beds that night.

It was a touching sight to see that motley collection of men, standing there before their tall Captain; he was strikingly handsome in his uniform with his keen blue eyes and kind face. The men stood there, each with a different kind of rifle, in all kinds and conditions of clothes, only the red and black arm-band and the same fine expression on their weatherbeaten faces common to all of them.

When the Captain ceased speaking, I was suddenly more conscious of the hush all around us, of the stillness of the fjord and of the awesome black mountains above us. It seemed a noble and fitting background for these humble, gallant men, braving the dark menace that now threatened their land. As all their lives they had challenged and fought the wild nature around them, so now with courage and scarcely more than their bare hands, they turned their faces to the storm. I turned to watch the fjord, and to stare at a tiny light that shone far in the distance, and a mouthful of raisins helped me to swallow the lump in my throat.

Soon we saw the first bus-load of soldiers drive off and then when the second was full, we gratefully took the seats they had kept for us. The cliffs were so high around us that there seemed to be no road ahead of us, but twisting and curving it stretched out to a wider valley beyond. Clinging to the side of the mountain, the bus slowly crept along by the dark lakes and deserted snowy hills, while we thanked our stars that we were not travelling that road on foot tonight.

We were warm and comfortable in the bus and were soon chatting with the friendly soldiers. I for one felt my confidence and spirits revive, for there is something about being in a skilfully driven vehicle that gives one the impression of danger left behind. Janet began to sing softly to herself and then, encouraged by the soldiers, was soon singing every Norwegian song she had learnt. At this time her voice was sweet and strong, and throughout the long ride she kept a smile on the faces of the passengers as they listened to her, many of them no doubt thinking of their own little daughters and sisters left at home.

'How old is she?' they all wanted to know. 'She's ten', George said, 'and has had rather a day!', though it was hard to credit it, seeing her merry face.

'Make her sing again', begged some voices at the back of the bus and so, the Norwegian repertoire being exhausted, we all joined her in English and plantation songs.

In this fashion we passed an hour or two of the journey and then silence descended on us as we all began to strain our eyes in the darkness for signs of civilisation, and to look at our watches. Nearly ten o'clock and we had no plans for the night.

At last we came to Odda, and after driving through the crowded Saturday night streets we stopped at the naval headquarters. We got out with the soldiers, and with them mounted some stairs and reached a large room filled with trestle tables and benches and great pile of brand-new steel helmets. We were greeted kindly by the officer in command, Captain—. Though looking rather pale and tired, he was impressively clean with spotless linen and a freshly scrubbed look. I suppose he had just come on night-duty fresh from a bath, but to me the impression he made was quite a shock, and I felt only too conscious of my grubbiness as I shook his immaculate hand.

A little later I learned that this officer (now safe in Little Norway) had recently been captured by the Germans, and only a few days previously had escaped with great daring and managed to rejoin his men. After showing us to a bench he went off with George and Stoddart to see what could be done for us. We sat and waited while a hurried meal was being prepared. When at last it was ready the soldiers fell to with gusto, and we too found places among them and began to eat. There was coffee, bread and cheese, cold meats and sausage, and gratefully we had our share. Then for another hour we sat about and waited. The children were weary now but, expecting to be moved every moment, I tried to keep them awake. The soldiers gradually departed, wishing us good luck, and soon we were left alone.

At last our Captain came back with our husbands. After great difficulty, for all the hotels were full, he had arranged for us to be taken to a private house for the night, and a car was now waiting to drive us there. George would come later as they still had things to discuss, so the children and I and the Stoddarts picked up our bundles, and once more walked out into the street.

The driver was told where to go and after a short drive we stopped at the gates of a large house. It certainly did not look like the humble home we had expected. I rang the bell wondering how to begin to introduce ourselves to strangers at this hour of the night. The door was opened by a short pleasant faced man with white hair – our host himself.

'Do you speak English?' I asked timidly, reluctant to start explanations in Norwegian. 'We have been sent by Captain—.'

'Yes I speak English', he said rather puzzled, 'but I am expecting only two naval officers.' But there we were, two women, one man and two children. It must have been rather overwhelming.

'Come in and welcome', he said and we followed him into a beautiful hall. It was obviously a very fine house. The walls were all panelled and lovely tapestries and burnished armour covered the walls. In front of the handsome fireplace, another man, a neighbour we learned, had risen to greet with some surprise the motley party that now advanced upon him. Hugging our disreputable parcels and sacks we tried to walk on tiptoe over the beautiful carpet.

I explained my missing husband and we all told them a little of what had happened to us that day. With a compassionate look at the two children, our host hurried away to rouse a servant and get beds prepared for us. By this time Simon and Janet were exhausted, and longing for bed, but they managed to keep upright in their impressive chairs and to laugh and smile and reply politely to questions. At last a maid came to say our rooms were ready, and the children and I followed our host upstairs, our heavy boots thudding on the polished wood. The Stoddarts both preferred to stay and talk over their whisky and sodas and wait until George arrived.

We were shown into two lovely large bedrooms, beautifully furnished with taste and luxury. Our host explained that his wife and daughters were away in Oslo, and that he was stranded at home alone waiting for their return.

The bath-water was hot, the beds were turned down ready for us. He modestly hoped that we would be comfortable! As we stood there in our skiing clothes, our faces smudged with fatigue and grime, our disgraceful bundles already defiling the spotless carpet, what could one say?

'Thank you – you are too kind to us.'

I have said as much for a dull evening, but there are no other words. Gratitude struck us almost dumb, but it certainly shone in the children's faces.

I heard George arrive just before one o'clock, and only then, when I knew we were both once more under the same roof and could hear the reassuring rumble of his voice downstairs, only then could I relax and drop off to sleep.

Chapter Thirteen

THE NEXT DAY, SUNDAY, WAS ALWAYS TO STAND OUT LATER IN our memories as an incongruous oasis of comfort in our humble wanderings. We were up early, for we were hungry, and the peaceful Sunday morning that we could see from our windows looked inviting. Our house was on a hill, so that we could look right over the small town to the lovely shore of the fjord which shone like a picture before us.

There was an electric fire in my room, an old-fashioned shape with a curved copper hood fixed to it. I lit the fire and had the idea of pressing a few garments by stretching them over the hot smooth surface. In this way I pressed my coat and skirt and Janet's dress and hair ribbons, and the white silk blouse bought a few days ago and never yet worn. When we descended the stairs in search of breakfast, the boys in clean shirts and ties, we really looked quite presentable again.

In the dining room we found a feast spread for us on a huge long table, and our host waiting for us. Our Russian, who once more was not on speaking terms with us, did not appear until the afternoon, but the rest of us did justice to the cold meats, fish and bacon and eggs.

This lovely room, both its long windows framing the view of the fjord, made a great impression on us. It was entirely white and pale blue. The floor-boards were enamelled white, and spotless white mats were placed here and there, and a large carpet under the table. The furniture was also white with pale blue cushions on the chairs, and the high walls were painted two shades of blue. A handsome white-tiled and brass stove stood in one corner, and polished brass ornaments gleamed on every side. The maid wore white from head to foot and silver shone on the table. This room must have been quite thirty feet long, and the effect with the sun pouring through the windows was utterly charming.

The children and I spent a long dream-like morning, roaming the garden with Herr M— our host, and soon felt we had been friends a long time. He was Swedish and the owner of a large chemical works here; we could just see his factory from the garden. At intervals throughout the morning we could hear an air-raid warning down in the bay; no-one took any notice of it and no aeroplanes appeared, so we sat out in the sunshine and just waited for the next meal. This was proving to be something of a problem for we had arrived on Saturday night and Herr M— had intended to pass the day with friends so that he had no provisions in the house. The servants spent the morning seeking for food, and George and Stoddart visited the naval headquarters again, so it was not until 3 pm that we had lunch, and then that we had the most exciting visitor.

Shortly before this, a small sea-plane had flown down into the fjord, and not long afterwards a young man wearing an airman's heavy flying outfit walked up to the front door. He proved to be an Englishman who had heard that we were there and had come to help us if he could. He was tall and dark, with startling blue eyes and long eyelashes, and a careless Oxford manner which greatly captivated Simon. We had scarcely time to be introduced to him when we trooped in to lunch, but during the meal he kept us very entertained with his stories. Gradually our first impression of a rather blasé charming young man changed into one of admiration.

Farragut as he was called, had left his university to be a stunt flyer in Hollywood, and seeking more excitement had flown a small aeroplane, first in Poland, and then in Finland against the Russians. In Poland, he said, the weather had been remarkable. Three weeks of cloudless days, and bright still moonlit nights. It had greatly favoured the Germans. In Finland he had become convinced that the Russian bombers were the most formidable and powerful in the world, and as yet nobody knew it. That war being over, he had been travelling back to England and had been caught at Oslo when the Germans landed. He escaped to fly again, this time for the Norwegians, but in a very different kind of machine. Farragut's description of this outdated sea-plane, and his efforts to drop his home-made bombs by raising the trap-door in the floor with a piece of string, had us all laughing.

The day before he had even flown over the village we had so lately left in a hurry, and because his machine went so slowly the Germans had not been able to hit him. It upset their calculations, he said, that anything could or would go so slowly in the air.

After lunch Herr M— opened a bottle of rare liqueur brandy, which we sipped in large glasses, while the men smoked his best cigars. Soon they had their maps out again, and helped by our new young friend who knew the countryside well, they eventually arranged a new plan of action.

The aeroplane was not big enough or strong enough to fly us to England. George at this time was considering whether to leave us and join with the Norwegians, so the problem as always was where to go next, for the Germans were slowly filtering over the countryside.

By now the British had landed and were fighting hard in the North, and the Norwegian army still had its headquarters at Voss. However, after our experiences the previous day, and conversations with the navy, who were continually being held back and told 'not to annoy the Germans', we were convinced that those headquarters were already under Quisling control.

At last the village of Øvre Eidfjord was decided upon, and our host telephoned to a small tourist hotel there, which was normally shut at this season. As Herr M— was well known and respected in these parts, the hotel owner promised to take us in for the night and we prepared to pack up our belongings. Then this best of men gave our family two much needed rucksacks, and knitted gloves which he had troubled to buy privately from the closed Sunday shops. With great joy I discarded my paper wrappings and sacks, and evolved two decent loads of all our belongings. I left a heap of discarded things for the kindly maid to dispose of, and at the last minute borrowed a much needed needle and reel of cotton from her.

So replenished and refreshed we said our heartfelt thanks and goodbyes to our friend; evening was already falling when we finally packed ourselves into the car the navy had lent us. George had been given a stamped and signed paper that morning,

Meeting Lars Saebe in Øvre Eidfjord.

enabling us to pass along the road which was now patrolled every few miles. As we skirted the fjord and our road crept round the mountain we saw a sea-plane skimming over the water. It was Farragut in his famous machine, and he waved to us as he gained height and flew off.

The road soon became so tortuous that Janet succumbed to car sickness, and we were held up several times, while I held my poor child's head by the roadside. It was beginning to get dark, and in my hurry, with one eye on our impatient driver, I left behind my only pair of gloves on a rock there. We sped on again, our signed paper enabling us to pass all the guards posted along the road, and after several hours we came to our destination. We got out and looked about us, and at once our car turned about and headed back for Odda. We were left in the dusk to make our own way.

George started off towards a large house with the signboard Eidfjord Gjestgjeveri over the porch, and we followed hesitatingly behind him. Then we saw a very tall man emerge from the shadow of the house where he had obviously been waiting for us. His long rugged face looked very serious and not at all glad to see us. He shook hands with George who began to explain that we were refugees from Bergen, but that we could pay for our food and board if he could kindly take us in. We others in the party said nothing as we fondly hoped that we looked like Norwegians and not like hunted Britishers. After a little more talk the man's face relaxed into a slight smile.

'Velkommen', he said, and turning led the way to his door. We followed him up the steps and, as we dumped our belongings on the floor, felt we had once again achieved a roof over our heads.

The whole hotel was in the process of being repainted, and apart from the kitchen where the family lived there was no place to sit. We hung about in the tiny hall, and examined the pictures and sheets of postcards for sale in the freshly drying dining-room. George left us there as soon as we were introduced. The only telephone in the village was in a shop some distance away and with our host he set out to find it.

At this time George was still undecided what to do; whether to leave his family and join up with the Norwegian naval forces, or whether to join Ulstrup who had a wild scheme to rush out to sea in a fast motor boat in the hope of eventually being picked up by a British ship. George felt it his duty to help if he could, but this evening the whole conversations by telephone with Voss, the Army headquarters, were so unsatisfactory that his suspicions were aroused and he decided to lie low for the present. It was as well he did, for we learned later that Quislings had practically taken over command there.

When George rejoined us we had already been shown to our bedrooms, which had been quickly prepared for us. There was only one room with a stove and I shamelessly installed myself and the children there. Our host soon had a fire going and as usual I washed a few essential socks, not knowing what the next day might bring forth, and hung them up to dry on the stove. After a plain supper of bread and cheese we went early to bed.

For the next two days we kept to the house and garden so as not to become known in the village. They were lovely spring days with the fruit trees almost ready to burst into blossom and the sky quite unclouded. But we couldn't keep our eyes from that serene sky.

Each morning, at the same hour, we would hear a heavy throbbing, and as the noise grew louder and louder until we were enveloped by it we would count the heavy German bombers

Små Lars Saebo – 'a fine man, our friend'.

passing over on their way to the North. Fifteen, twenty, twenty-three! We would remember and count hopefully when they returned the same evening. I don't remember that there was ever one missing, and we feared for our British forces.

During these days, while the children had a lovely time playing with a herd of thirty newly born goats, and I washed clothes and hair, and got our belongings into fine shape again, and the Stoddarts kept long hours in their room, George made fast friends with the hotel keeper, Lars Saebø. He was an enormous man – quite six foot four inches tall and, as he told us later on, with the longest arm-stretch in Norway; but because his father had been called Big Lars, he was known still as Little Lars. His long rugged face, with its keen blue eyes and stern jutting jaw, was transformed when he smiled, and in many a long talk he revealed a gentleness and a strength of character which completely won our confidence. While he did various jobs in the farmyard our family followed him about enthralled, while in rusty English he told us something of his life.

As a small boy he had a hard time crossing the mountains, alone and in all weathers, in sole charge of many laden pack-horses. Then later he had tried his fortune in the States, but to his old father's joy he had come back to his own land about twelve years before and had taken over and improved the old guest-house. Now he was a leading man in the village and, we felt instinctively, a man to be trusted.

George and Stoddart agreed to tell him our story and ask his advice and help. Naturally Små Lars had many relatives in these parts, and he knew every track and valley in the surrounding countryside. In case the Germans came nearer we needed to have our next move planned and ready. All one long afternoon the three men sat with maps before them, discussing and discarding one idea after another until the final plan was decided on, and if a hasty move should be necessary we knew where to make for.

Farragut had flown over to see us the first day here, and had advised that we could not do better than hide in some distant saeter or tourist hut in the mountains. He was leaving for the north that day and would try to get through to England and tell them of our plight.

We never heard from him again, but months later learned that he had been shot down in his pathetic plane, but he had eventually turned up in British lines leading several German prisoners with him.

For us however our only means of escape was to walk, and for the present, when the Germans were on the move every day, to keep ourselves hidden. So we planned to set off in a day or two over the mountains to a tourist hut many thousands of feet up, but in case of sudden danger we would not be able to use the rough road, but would have to climb a gorge to get away secretly.

On our third night here, when I came downstairs after tucking the children up, I was met by worried faces. A message had just come through. The naval forces had left Odda that morning and the town had since been taken over by the Germans. As the town was only an hour or two distant it was imperative that we get away at once, and so I packed our haversacks, and at the last possible moment wakened the sleeping children. Half drugged with sleep, it was a sad business getting them into their clothes, but in only a few minutes we were all gathered in the hall waiting for Små Lars to set us upon the road. His wife gave me a much needed pair of gloves, and thanking her for the many kind things she had done for us we followed her husband into the night.

It seemed pitch dark to our unaccustomed eyes, and a warm wind fanned our faces as we stepped out into the garden. Through the garden and the orchard we followed and then climbed a hedge, crossed over two rough fields and then climbed a low wall. We found ourselves before a darkened house, and telling us not to make a sound, for he did not want the other villagers to know the road we must take, Små Lars left us and knocked to wake up the house. After a short time, while we waited in eerie silence, he emerged out of the darkness and beckoned us to follow him. Then in a few whispered words he told us that he had not been able to get the key of the tourist hut he had in mind, but in any case we must get out of the valley at once.

Then began a terrific climb up a rocky winding path, which skirted deep chasms and wound forever upward. Små Lars went ahead, carrying a lantern, his white rubber boots gleaming in the light and helping the first follower to step exactly in his foot-steps. There were loose stones, pools and slippery ice, but we managed to keep up with our guide and scramble after him. A waterfall made a deep gorge on our right-hand side, but in the darkness we could not, fortunately, see how far below us it fell. We were all very out of breath as we strained ourselves to go forward at a good pace, and George suffered considerably because his boots were too small for him and every time he stubbed his toe he was in agony. After an hour, our silent guide sat down on a rock, and we gathered about him to ask if we were nearly there.

'Not half way yet', he said smiling. 'Another two hours at this rate.'

It appears we had been travelling slowly, while I had been under the impression that we were fairly skimming along. At least my feet seemed to float ahead on their own volition for I could scarcely see

'Små Lars went ahead carrying a lantern'.

where I placed them or feel very much in my thick boots and socks. The children, being in fine condition, had felt it easier going than we did. Just after three hours climbing, the mountain path opened into a narrow valley, and perched on the hill-side, half hidden by enormous boulders, we saw the little house we were seeking. It belonged to Små Lars' sister, and he thought that she would take us in.

Six extra people in that little shack! In silence we crept up to the wooden steps in front of the house, and looked about us while Små Lars knocked discreetly at the door. We could now distinguish four or five small houses growing haphazardly out of the steep mountain side, while a sheer high cliff ran the whole opposite length of the valley. It was the beautiful village of Hjølmo.

After a minute or two, a figure opened the door and Små Lars slipped inside. Almost at once he appeared and beckoned us to follow him. We all filed into a large living room where the owner of the house, a small stocky man, waited to greet us. He looked rather apprehensive, as well he might, for there were so many of us, and he must have had a surprise awakening. Just then Små Lars' sister entered the room. She was tall and pale. Her dark hair hung in two long pig-tails and she had hastily wrapped herself in a long coat. In a few words Små Lars introduced us, and with a shy smile she extended both hands to us

'Velkommen', she said.

Without more ado, she started off to find us bedding, and in a short time we had all been given something for the night. The Stoddarts were allotted a large divan bed in the living room, while our family took over a small bedroom containing three beds. We put the children in the two single beds, and with some trepidation George and I crawled into a short box bed. It was incredibly hard, and full of mysterious bumps, but at least we could lie down. So, still in our clothes, we drew the rough blankets up to our chins, and 2.30 am came and found us all asleep in our new refuge.

Chapter Fourteen

NEXT MORNING WE WERE UP EARLY, CURIOUS TO SEE THE village by daylight. Three or four houses clung to the mountainside, a path of stones like a river-bed forming a rough path from house to house. The biggest building of all was a barn evidently used by all the families, where some baby goats and cows were kept. Other goats dotted the mountainside and clustered round the doorways in search of scraps.

That morning we saw them having a very unusual meal; the little granddaughter of the house was, like every other child in the district, revelling in the glut of oranges, and the goats were enjoying the orange peel. During the next few days the little girl and the goats kept up the feast from dawn to dark.

Now we got to know our hosts, and, Små Lars having gone home again long before we were up, we had to make ourselves understood as best we could. The dialect here was very different from Bergensk, and in many ways resembled Swedish. Madelene, Sma Lars' sister, soon became our close friend, and learning that she had lately been ill, we soon arranged a routine to spare her any extra work. Apart from a little more meat in the 'lapskaus' (stew with potatoes), the staple dish, and more bread-making for the six extra mouths, there was nothing more for her to do. We laid and cleared away every meal and took turns among ourselves for all the washing up. We cleaned our rooms, made our beds and hoped we were no trouble. As always I was kept busy washing our small supply of clothes and keeping our possessions ship-shape in our haversacks.

There were three or four little children in the village, and Janet was soon up at their house playing hopscotch, and sharing bread and jam. They hadn't seen hopscotch before, but soon enjoyed it.

On our second day, having arranged a price to pay our hosts, we cast about to find more money. When George had telephoned the army headquarters at Voss, he had also learned that his Captain, whom we had last seen striding out of Bergen, was there also with his wife who had been spending a holiday nearby. Now we thought that he would probably be able to draw money for us, and so we asked our host if he knew anyone who would take a message to him. He suggested someone at once; the very man for us, he said, had just arrived back in the village and he would fetch him. And so it was we met Sylfest Myklatun for the first time.

Tall and powerful, with a strong face and keen twinkling blue eyes, he turned out to be the father of the four lovely children who played with Simon and Janet. He could speak a little English, for he too had spent some years in the States and then came home to settle down with a Norwegian wife. George, feeling instinctively that he was a man to be trusted, told him our story and asked for help. Sylfest had some knowledge of the route we must take, and with the help of our map they considered the chances of success. It would be a hard and strenuous journey over high mountains on skis nearly all the way, and we reckoned that it would be at least four days before we could expect our messenger back again. For a small sum, for he was a poor man, Sylfest offered to undertake it. George wrote a letter to the Captain, asking for money and wishing him luck, and as we had no envelopes, I sewed the letter up in another piece of paper.

So Sylfest set off and we waited for his return. On Sunday, 26th April, Simon's thirteenth birthday, we all had a cup of coffee to celebrate. George and I and the children sat in the cosy kitchen chatting with Madelene, and watching her make potato bread. It was so fascinating that George soon coaxed her into letting him take over the baking and enjoyed himself hugely. Cold boiled potatoes were mixed with an equal quantity of raw flour, and then kneaded and rolled out as thinly as possible with a dented rolling pin. Then the flat top of the kitchen stove was wiped clean, and the thin dough spread upon it. It was quite an art to turn it over and

Cecilia (Sella) Myklatun

then fold it into four when it was finished. Madelene was vastly amused by George's antics, and we all spent a merry afternoon encouraging him.

There was little hard bread in the village and so we ate a lot of this potato cake, which though it started crisp, eventually grew limp like a pancake. We had enough to eat, but not much variety, potatoes and goats' cheese appearing at every meal. The families here grew their own potatoes, and the cheese was made in a rough shed near the house. We watched a young girl making some on a low ring-stove; first the white soapy goats' cheese, and then the more complicated hard brown cheese which keeps forever. It has a very sharp yet sweet flavour, and we fortunately grew to like it very much, for later we were to have little else to live on. We filled

Sylfast A. Myklatun

in the next three days of waiting clambering with the goats over the rocky hillsides, walking down the partly dried river bed and just standing about waiting for news.

Our messenger returned a day sooner than we had expected. He had a note for us, but no money. He told us that just as he had located the Captain, the Germans had bombed the town, and so the Captain and his Swedish wife had decided to come back with him on skis, to share our hiding place! He had left them in a nearby village for the night, and had come on ahead to tell us. We had not expected this, and we were rather dismayed to think that yet another couple was added to our group. Sylfest seemed rather worried too, and later we learned they had told the villagers who put them up that they were English, and that we were hiding with

Sylfest. When our host, who had never shown as much enthusiasm for us as did his wife, heard this, he became very nervous and all that night we heard him and Madelene talking urgently together. It was not until the early hours that the anxious talk ceased.

Now we knew that soon the whole countryside would know of our whereabouts, and we were placing our friends in grave danger by remaining with them. Next day the Captain and his wife arrived, very tired and anxious after their long hurried trip. The Captain was a tall thin irascible man, who had kept our small English colony in Bergen in a continual state of tension with his bitter feuds with so many of his associates. His wife, who was known as Dokken, did really look like an over-stuffed doll, with bright golden hair rigidly waved over her broad cheeks. They had always been friendly with us and the Stoddarts, mostly because they had quarrelled with everyone else. However, here they were, and they spent the night in a house in the village.

Next morning George and Stoddart, weary of hanging about doing nothing, decided to work on the rather neglected potato fields. They had bought overalls in the village, and now together with Simon they started to carry down loads of manure, and to clear stones from the rough fields. Meanwhile Janet and I visited another house in the village, where lived an old couple, brother and sister. One small room was completely filled by a weaving loom, and a bolt of cloth was in the process of being woven. Any spare moment she had, this cheerful little woman would leap into the seat and then, pedalling and throwing the shuttle back and forth at an amazing speed, weave a few more inches of cloth. It was wonderful stuff, like Scots tweed, but of more sober colours, mostly black and white.

We were fascinated watching her and fingering the many different patterns she had stocked about the room. I wanted to buy something for Janet, because now her green wool dress was torn in many places and worn threadbare behind. I bought a metre of grey vadmel, and was just fixing the price and borrowing a reel of black cotton when George rushed in.

'We must leave at once!' he gasped out. 'Germans are coming up the pass!'

We ran with him out of the house to our own rooms, where we found our dear Madelene in tears. In frantic haste, we darted here and there packing our rucksacks, fearful of leaving the smallest

Leaving Hjølmo.

incriminating thing behind us. Sylfest was waiting for us when five minutes later we hurried out of the house up the hill. The children ran with their bundles, and soon we were all scrambling over the rocks in his wake. As we dashed after our guide I felt such a weakness in my knees as never before, and my thumping heart made the blood sing in my ears. We had to strain to keep Sylfest in sight.

A few hundred yards from the village, he motioned us to keep hidden, and in a crouching fearful manner he skirted round a hillock to look down on the gorge. As yet no-one was in sight, and so in awful silence and fear we followed him, half doubled up, and darting about so as not to be seen leaving. This sudden flight was quite one of our worst moments, because the shock of it had weakened our legs, and yet we had to travel as fast as ever we could force ourselves. The two children kept close on Sylfest's heels, Simon carrying a heavy rucksack, and Janet's teddy-bear having a good view of everything.

We kept on until well away from the village, and following our guide we crashed through some trees to look down on an old stone quarry. It was filled with mighty boulders, and Sylfest led us to a cleverly concealed hiding place under a great rock. We all squeezed inside, pushing our bundles in front of us, and there in the quiet and dark we were left to recover our breath. When he had seen us safely stowed away, Sylfest told us to remain there quietly until he came again, and then he left us to return to his home.

For perhaps an hour we sat there, not making a sound, expecting any moment to hear the voices of a search party. Then as nothing happened we squeezed out in ones and twos to the mouth of the cave for a breather, while we kept our eyes and ears alert. Janet who was the smallest was wedged furthest into the cave, with rock only inches from her face. We must have been under our rock two hours or more, when we heard whistles, and to our great relief we saw two familiar figures coming through the trees. Then Sylfest leaned into the cave and told us to come out as there were as yet no Germans in the village. The figures which had been sighted coming up the gorge, and which had caused such alarm, had been only Norwegian lads who had come to warn us that Germans had moved into the village below, and had taken over the hotel where we had so lately stayed with Små Lars. He was even now settling the officers into the rooms we had used.

With much relief we came out of our hiding place, stretched our legs and smiled encouragingly at each other. It was good to be moving again and to see the large baskets of food which our friends had brought with them. When we removed the clean napkins we discovered two large dishes of hot meat balls and potatoes, and hunks of bread and strawberries! It was a lovely meal and a welcome gift from two village families.

We ate with gratitude while once more we planned our next step. At last it was decided that we should all start off at once to climb the mountain up to snow-level, following a clearly defined track, while the village men went back to their homes to get blankets and food for us. We set off in single file in fine spirits, climbing at a good pace for about two hours until we reached snow-level. Here the Captain solemnly took the lead and we followed, slowing down our pace to his more cautious footsteps.

Soon we arrived at the summit where the snow was deep and soft. We plunged on, only to find ourselves up to our waists in half-melted snow, and had the greatest difficulty in pulling each leg after us. We saw two pairs of skis propped against a steep rock on our right, but as there was nothing to fasten them onto our feet with, and no sticks, we had to give up the idea of using them. So we floundered on, the daylight beginning to fade and the snow becoming deeper and softer as we progressed. After about only twenty yards in half an hour of sinking up to our waists with every step we were all completely bogged. We found out later that we were over a frozen river bed; at the time it was quite alarming to sink so deeply into the snow.

After an hour of struggling we had not gone fifty yards, but stuck as we were, we were reluctant to retrace our steps. In this sorry state our good friends found us when they appeared carrying several pairs of skis and weighty haversacks. Our trusted Sylfest was now accompanied by three other men. One was a nameless young man who we were never to see again, another his brother-in-law, sturdy, cherry-faced and with red hair, who was to help us faithfully during the next two months. The third man was a little dried-up fellow with a long drooping moustache and a thin neck, Sylfest's father-in-law 'Father William', who was to become a trusted friend. We felt greatly comforted to see them, and especially admired the old man coming to our aid.

'It was a lovely meal'.

'Oh him', said Sylfest. 'He dances on skis and knows every stick and stone on these mountains!'

There were not enough skis for all of us, but Stoddart, George, Simon and myself were soon fitted up. The problem of how to fasten the primitive skis was soon solved. Father William quickly cut some young twigs, and peeling off the bark he used it like wire to tie each of our feet to the skis. It was quite effective and following the rest of the party, who had been similarly treated, I soon caught them up. Janet had no skis, but Sylfest produced from his pockets a pair of thick black stockings and some woollen knickers for her. He pulled the stockings over her boots and so, helped by him, she was able to struggle along behind us.

Some of the others had no skis at this time, but I don't remember exactly how we distributed them. I kept mine, following Simon who had shot ahead, until we came to a steep hill, and then after most difficult struggles I handed them over to someone else. Janet crept on hands and knees until the black stockings split down the front with wear. Our 'friendly' Russian forbade her to follow in her tracks, which would have been easier. Janet was well behind when Sylfest came and rescued her, carrying her standing in front of him on his skis, until they caught me up.

From then on Janet and I went on foot, or rather on hands and knees, and the more tired we became the more comic it seemed to us. At some places the snow had melted completely and we advanced at a good rate over ground covered with blue-berries. Then as we got higher there was only deep snow, and the skiers got well ahead of us. It is hard to remember how the time passed as we pressed stubbornly on. We had started off at about 2.30 pm, and it was 9.30 pm and dark before we eventually reached the hut we were making for. For an hour or two Janet and I crawled on hands and knees, it being the only way to move at all in the soft snow. At one time, Sylfest, who had been helping those ahead, came back and gave me his huge leather mittens which were a great help. It was not bad fun and often Janet and I, struck by the ludicrous side of it, would roll over in fits of weak laughter, but for the most part we plodded on grimly enough. One really never knows how a fantastic situation is going to strike you. Was it actually us, climbing a Norwegian mountain on hands and knees?

It was getting dark and there was not a living thing in sight –

'There was only deep snow'.

only the quiet billowing hills and the track we followed in the snow.

'I really don't believe it', Janet had said, between pants. I had a brilliant and comforting idea.

'Think what a help it will be to you at school. You will never be at a loss for something to write about. "My Adventure in The Snow", "Lost On a Mountain", "My Most Exciting Experience". You will be able to work it into anything! Most of your friends have scarcely been out after dark.' So we cheerfully floundered on, our trivial conversation and the hard exercise keeping at bay the full realisation of the danger and discomfort. We found it wiser to keep well ahead of our other female companions, who as time went on grew more tearful and dispirited.

At last we climbed the last hillock and were over the top. Then came an easier stage on firm snow, for it was colder up here, and then the good moment when a speck in the distance, or rather a fold in the snowy hills, could be pointed out to us as our destination. Simon, carrying a full pack, and two villagers were already out of sight, rushing ahead to open up our frozen lodging, when we started on the last few miles. Sylfest now lifted Janet up and carrying her pick-a-back he took her the whole way home. Then I climbed onto the skis of the Captain's wife, who had caught us up, and holding her waist, we both walked smoothly over the snow.

George was close beside us when we suddenly saw to our surprise a snow covered hut emerge out of the white landscape. This was to be our home for a week, but a week when every day was like a month.

Chapter Fifteen

THE FIRST ARRIVALS HAD ALREADY GOT THE FIRE GOING WHEN we crossed the threshold. We passed through one room, thick with ice and crowded with logs and cast-off implements, and entered another room where two bunks, a table and an iron stove were the sole furnishings. Sticks blazed in the stove and a large pot of snow had been put on the fire to melt. We knew that it was dangerous to drink it, but we had such parching thirst that we drank cupfuls of it as soon as there was enough melted to scoop into a cup.

My first thought was to get Janet's soaking clothes off and put her to bed. I peeled off her boots and torn stockings and wet clothes, and with two blankets climbed up to the upper bunk to make a bed. It was filled with hay, and after tossing it about a little, it soon seemed a most inviting bed. I helped her up out of the way of the ten other weary people crowding the hut, pulled a dry jersey over her underclothes and tucked the blankets round her. Then I found a foothold on the wobbling plank which had been placed on the icy floor and dragged off my soaking boots.

With the exercise we were all quite warm and now, with our thirst quenched, we felt fine. Our village friends now unpacked an incredible amount of food and blankets which they had carried for us, and soon we were drinking tea and eating bread and sausage. I passed up sandwiches to a cheerful Janet who looked cosily down from her high perch, perfectly delighted with the picnic. As things turned out, except for brief excursions out of doors, she had to spend almost the whole week aloft, as in our tiny room it was the only place she could play.

The meal finished, our friends from the village shouldered their empty rucksacks and set off for their homes again, promising to come up in a day or two if it should be safe for them to slip away. And so we stood at the door of our new home and watched them disappear into the night.

Now the problem was how to distribute eight people into two narrow bunks. Simon soon joined Janet in the top one, and George and I would have to find room there later. The bottom bunk also had hay and plenty of blankets, so the other two couples agreed to share it in shifts through the night. On the floor of the hut they rigged up another rough bed with the table and some planks and, stoking up the fire as best we could, we prepared to settle down.

The Captain and his wife took the lower bunk and the Stoddarts settled with many blankets on the upturned table on the floor. I crawled in amongst the children and we were as tight as sardines. When George tried to squeeze himself in, the only solution seemed for both of us to sit upright at each end, the children head to tail in the middle. Three in a bunk is the height of discomfort, but four is just pure torture. The great difficulty was to be quiet, for even a whisper or stifled yelp of pain when we tried to ease our cramps was naturally very irritating for others. It was hard for all of us and the tension can be imagined.

Oddly enough we suffered most from the heat of the stove and the tobacco smoke whilst our friends below shivered with cold! When morning came, George and I, having taken it in turns to sit on the only available chair, had had no sleep at all, and the others only an hour or two.

We spent exactly one week in the hut and the whole time we had two great problems – the lack of space and the iron rations we had to live on. Our friends came up every few days, but we were never sure if or when they could ever come again, so we had to eat as little as possible, in order to leave something in reserve.

We had a saucer of porridge with a little tinned milk for breakfast. Then for lunch we had one tin of meat or fish balls between us all and a potato each. We had two thin 'Marie' biscuits for tea and a slice of bread with a sardine or a slice of sausage for supper. As the children were always ravenous, George always shared his food with Simon and I mine with Janet.

The first day we had a great scare when we heard the sound of hundreds of feet coming over the hills and a man's voice shouting. We sat frozen with fright thinking that German soldiers had discovered us. Then as we sat petrified, surrounded by noise of stamping feet and barking dogs, came a knock at the door. With signs we persuaded the Captain's Swedish wife to answer it. After we had waited many anxious minutes listening to their unintelligible conversation, she at last closed the door. It had turned out to be only a harmless man following a herd of reindeer, who had expected to spend the night in our hut. They passed on over the valley and we relaxed in relief, but from then on we spoke to each other in whispers, afraid that our voices might carry far over the silent snow.

After that first impossible night, Simon determined to fix himself a bed, and by the end of the day had achieved an ingenious hammock. With an axe he painfully cut wire netting into a strip long enough for a bed, and with wire found on a fence he managed to suspend the whole contraption from the ceiling, high over our heads. It was a physical feat to get into it and, once in, he had to lie perfectly still, for the slightest creak was disturbing. Even turning over a little was enough to irritate our nervy friends, but so eager were we to make ourselves unobtrusive that Simon never moved all night, and Janet could be viciously jabbed by both of us in the night and a more or less noiseless gasp was the only reaction. However, as can be imagined, we were anxious to find another place for ourselves as the whole situation was becoming too much of a strain.

The men were kept busy cutting down trees and sawing up firewood, while we women shared the cooking and washing up. We remained long hours indoors, talking in whispers and playing endless games of patience. We were continually frozen with fear when our friends heard aeroplanes or imagined figures in the distance. Often we would spend hours motionless because the Captain's Swedish wife was sure she heard footsteps approaching.

Janet, sitting aloft, cutting out pictures from old magazines found in the hut, annoyed them almost to frenzy when she unconsciously gave a cheerful hum or chuckle. So the second time Sylfest came up George asked him if he could not move our family to another similar hut which we could see across the valley, and he promised to arrange it. It made us laugh later to learn that the others had asked him to move us too.

The Captain, who had been very shaken by his experiences, slept in all his clothes and seldom spoke. He once startled us all by yelling at George,

'Take your damned children out of here!'

George asked what he objected to.

'The boy is fine, but the girl is too cheerful', he grunted.

George, rather roused, appealed to all, saying,

'You must admit they've both been good, not a whimper or a tear from either of them since the start. Many little girls might be making a fine fuss by this time.'

'Better if she did cry a bit', said the poor harassed man. 'She's just too damned cheerful. It's unnatural.' He once threatened Janet with,

'Cry can't you? Don't you realise you'll soon be killed?'

After this, we did not allow Janet to speak at all in the hut. She played silent games in her bed, and kept her conversation for our brief trips outside.

When we opened our door on the seventh morning, we found ourselves lost in a dense mist. It was so thick that we had given up hope of anyone visiting us that day; then to our joy we saw the familiar figures of Sylfest, his red-haired brother-in-law and the younger helper, approaching on skis. They had come to move our family across the valley and our inward elation can be imagined. We happily packed our belongings while they drank tea and divided the provisions fairly between us all; we bade a friendly goodbye to our companions. On seeing us depart their spirits also rose and they were as cheered as we were at the easing of the situation. Gratefully we followed our guides over the soft snow through the mist.

I took up the rear of the procession, noticing how Janet's legs were as thin as sticks from sitting in her bunk all these days – and mine too felt wobbly with lack of exercise and short rations, but I never remember feeling happier. We grinned at each other through the damp and plodded on. We came at last to a deep river which cut the valley in two. It was just beginning to be swollen with the melting snows and only at one point could we hope to cross it. Two men leapt over the rushing water and then Sylfest helped us each in turn, tying a thick rope around our waists and

'The first hut on our own'.

throwing the end to the others. With a good jump we all landed safely, and climbed a hill after our guides. When at last we came to our stone hut, a fire was already roaring in the stove; we dumped our packs and leaned against the walls, surveying our new home with vast appreciation.

There were two narrow bunks, and two packing cases, but the floor was covered with ice about six inches deep. Sylfest had brought plates and cups, and a kettle, and we soon had water on the stove for tea. They had also brought us bread, potatoes, a side of bacon, a hard sausage, and many tins of meat and sardines. The two other men went off into the mist again and in a short while returned carrying armfuls of birch twigs which they stuffed into our bunks.

Outside we watched them chop expertly the trees they had felled and dragged from the woods nearby, and soon our beds were full of wet springy twigs, and the rest of the trees were chopped into logs for the fire. They now produced two waterproof sheets, which they spread over the twigs, and from a large bundle brought forth four thick blankets. Our astonishment and

The interior of 'our little home'.

admiration for our good friends was so complete, that we all felt a choking gratitude, and a slightly crazy happiness swept over us.

I made our helpers a pile of sandwiches and tea, and while they ate we laughed and chatted in a very merry fashion until it was time for them to leave. It was dark when at last they buckled on their empty packs and skis, and with friendly shouts melted into the night for their long journey home again. Our happy fit continued and we hugged each other with abandon, and wrapped our little home close round us.

'Tonight', I said, 'there will be no rations – a blow out for one and all!' And for the first time for a week we did not count the slices of bread, but made a fine stew of potatoes and a whole tin of meat balls.

Full at last, we set about getting into bed. They seemed marvellously comfortable and springy at first, but so narrow that we put Janet in with George and Simon with me. Even then one leg had to hang over the side to make enough room.

We were so happy that we kept each other awake by ever funnier remarks until even the teddy-bear awoke to life, and from then onwards had a separate existence of his own. He piped up with many cheeky remarks, which Janet would have hesitated to risk, and only George's half stern,

'Pipe down, all of you', effectively stopped our hilariousness. We were all quiet at last; we said a prayer together for all our many blessings and so, feeling securely at anchor amidst the vast sea of snow, we slept.

A few hours later we were startled wide awake by a loud crack of splitting wood, and the bed occupied by George and Janet collapsed in the middle. They were so tired, and as there was no remedy for it, they spend the rest of the night making the best of it – their middles very near the ice on the floor and their legs in the air. Meanwhile Simon and I had found our inviting bed a rather painful delusion. As the night wore on, the young twigs sank lower in our mattress, and the bare hard branches and pointed sticks turned our bed into a rack. However we all slept some part of the night and awoke at daylight grateful to think that our new abode was no dream, and that we could please ourselves in all things.

Simon was soon out of bed, stepping carefully into his boots left by the bedside, and picking his way over the mud, he opened the door. Lying in my bunk I could see the wide hills in the distance, and the snow coming up to the doorstep.

In the late spring and summer our hut was used by the people of the village who would bring up their goats and sheep to the fresh grass. Our stove would be used for the making of goat's cheese, and was specially made low and flat with the top consisting of about a dozen interlocking rings.

Expertly, for by this time he had had plenty of practice, Simon now lit the stove and put the kettle on. After he had washed, he served us all a cup of tea in bed, and started to cut large slices off our side of bacon. We had no frying pan, but we found a small 'witch's cauldron' hanging on a nail, and Simon soon had this clean and the appetising smell of bacon was filling the hut by the time we had slipped into our boots, washed outside in a bucket of icy water, and started laying our breakfast table on the two packing cases.

Breakfast finished we strolled, well pleased with ourselves, into the sun and surveyed our surroundings. Far in the distance we could see the hut we had left the day before, and a thin puff of blue smoke showed that they were also stirring. A thick wood of low twisted birch trees lay at our backs and a meeting of streams cut a deep gully through the snow not far from the house.

Heating water in the cauldron, I washed up and set about the complicated task of making our beds. The twigs must be taken out and repacked, and the muddy floor made it a difficult job. George's bunk looked as if a small charge of dynamite had exploded in it, for the wood was rotten, and now the bunk had no floor to it. A few hundred yards away on our hillside we saw another deserted hut, larger and better built than ours. Simon and George went off to explore and soon returned carrying a stout plank between them. With three planks salvaged in this way they managed to mend the bed, resting the long ends which jutted out on a high packing case, so making an extra bench for our pail of water and tea-cups.

All that day we worked hard, rigging up pegs for our haversacks and a neat two-tiered cupboard for our plates. We ate well, because it was our wedding anniversary, making the most of our provisions and making endless cups of tea. Because we had so little tea, (only a two-ounce packet) and it being rationed and hard to come by, we invented a way of using it very economically. We boiled water in the kettle and added a little tea, then when we next wanted to drink we filled it up again with water and brought it to the boil; then we added a pinch more tea and it was strong enough to drink. We went on in this way, never removing the tea leaves until days later when the kettle would be almost full and there was no room for more water. In this way two ounces lasted us a week.

The second day in our hut was bitterly cold, with a piercing wind whistling through every crack between the large stones which formed the walls. It blew George's hair about indoors! Janet and I spent the entire day gathering long wet sphagnum moss in our skirts and the boys stuffed it into the cracks as deeply as they could. When we had finished the inside (and very pretty the green and red moss looked) we started on the outside, and only at dark did we stop to nurse our cold and aching fingers; but that night the hut was warm, and the wind and rain outside meant nothing to us.

Sylfest paid us a surprise visit the next day, arriving at dusk and giving us rather a fright. We had a meal together and a good talk.

He had brought us more food – bread that his wife had baked and welcome potatoes and butter. Kindest of all, he had brought Janet more warm stockings, and fine warm wool cardigan for me.

A few days later, on Easter Sunday, we had an early visit from Små Lars and his wife. They brought us, amongst other luxuries, several tall jars of stewed fruit and a precious jar of pork chops in jelly. We had a meal together and had a lovely long talk, hearing all the news of the Germans in the village and the meagre news which they had got over the radio. The British at this time were preparing to leave Norway to her fate and our disappointment can be imagined. Små Lars had German officers billeted in his house and there were about sixty soldiers in the school house, spending money like water. They bought butter and ate it in the streets with spoons or fingers, like ice cream. Everything in consequence was getting scarce and Små Lars had only managed to get a few packets of cigarettes for us. Our party, the eight of us, had been 'distributed' between two or three families when they applied for rations. Sylfest and his sister had added us to their sons and daughters and so they were able to feed us.

Later in the afternoon Små Lars managed to cross the river and with his pack half full of presents paid a short visit to our friends in the other hut. His wife stayed on with us until he came back, and it was not until dusk that they set off home again.

We had a grand talk together and became better friends than ever. On leaving Små Lars said,

'Don't get down-hearted.'

'There's no fear of that – we're perfectly happy', I said truthfully 'and enjoying ourselves.'

'Well, hardly that', smiled Små Lars, 'but I can see you're in good spirits.'

Chapter Sixteen

FOR DAYS AFTER THIS WE HAD NO WORD FROM ANYONE, AND WE were beginning to look over our stocks of food and ration ourselves. Then one afternoon came a timid knock on the door and we discovered three smiling small boys, laden with bulging knapsacks. They were Sylfest's two sons and a cousin, who had struggled all this way with an incredibly heavy load of potatoes, bread and sardines for us. I fed them with sandwiches while George tried to get them to talk. We were always frantic for news of the war, but they had nothing to tell us and soon escaped outside, where they dug out a little sledge from an out-house nearby.

Soon all five children were careering down the slopes, their shouts and laughter sounding strangely amid the quiet. The visitors seemed unwilling to start homewards again but at last, after I presented each with a bar of precious chocolate, they made polite goodbyes and started off. After this they regularly came up to see us, once bringing their two little sisters of eight and ten years old, each duly laden with a bundle or a can of milk. On that occasion they spent almost the whole day with us, but left reluctantly before dusk.

Meanwhile we lived our ordinary routine from day to day. My work consisted of endless washing dishes and scouring the only pot, washing clothes in icy water that made me leap about with the pain in my hands, making the complicated beds, and keeping our humble home ship-shape. I really enjoyed it. It was not unlike

Lars, Arne and Endre from Hjølmo.

playing 'house', with twigs tied on a stick for a broom, boxes for tables, a cup apiece, a bucket to wash in and a pungent wood stove to cook on. About every other night I heated a full cauldron of water and one or two of us had a bath in sections, and changed our underclothes. We had one change apiece, but as we slept in them we had to change them often. Fortunately, in the bright sun and wind, things dried quickly and our whites were bleached with little labour.

One day George and Simon dammed the little stream which ran nearby and which every day made a fuller, deeper channel in the snow. Every morning the boys would run out in their underclothes and then have a quick bath in the icy water. Janet and I remained faithful to the warm bath in the hut. Once we lost count of the days of the week, and thinking it was Saturday we had a grand clean up, making ourselves and the hut spick and span and laying in neat stocks of wood and kindling. Next day, idly enjoying our Sunday, we were happy to see Sylfest approaching bearing gifts as usual. Then we learned it was really Saturday.

Sylfest brought us a large dry salted fish, which we took up to the dam and left in the water for several days; even then it had a strong salty smell. I decided to mix it with potatoes for fish cakes, and spent a long time picking the meat from the numberless bones and mixing it with mashed potatoes. They were good, but hardly worth the mess I made of every plate and spoon in the process.

In bad weather when all our household chores were finished, there were long hours which had to be spent somehow quietly in the hut. Janet and George between them remembered by trial and error how to make a draughts and ludo board, and with a sheet of paper and pencil and some Norwegian coins they managed to have many an exciting game. With cardboard from our tea packets we also laboriously made a pack of cards.

Now often we would be engrossed in a game when we would be startled by a sudden knock on our door. Sometimes it was our friends, but often George would open the door to a stranger. On these occasions the children and I did not say a word, but left all the conversation to George, who spoke the language more convincingly. These stray callers, crossing the mountain from one village to another, were accustomed to spend an hour or two making tea in the various huts on the way. We always gave them tea and a sandwich and, probably wondering deeply but having refrained from asking us questions, they would go on their way.

About this time Janet's bright green dress became so torn and threadbare, her elbows with large holes, the skirt sadly worn behind, that I started to make her another out of the grey vadmel I had bought in such a hurry in the village below. I cut it out with our nail scissors, making a skirt with a pleat in front, and a pinafore top with the last inches left over. I unpicked the green binding which had finished off the hem of her old dress and used this to give a pretty laced-up effect to the little bodice. I had a darning needle and black thread, but the stuff was so thick that my back-stitching looked almost like machine work when finished.

With her old frock I made a tiny pair of trousers with braces for the teddy-bear and kept these for Janet's eleventh birthday on 28th May. George and Simon had also been busy for the celebration. George sawed and shaped a square of wood into the size of a chequer board and, with a penknife and ink, made a very fine draughts board on one side and a ludo board on the other. Simon took a piece of birch wood and hollowed and carved it into a dice box, complete with lid. The dice itself took a long time to make (and always seemed to show 2) but all was ready in time for us all to wish her a happy birthday when the day came. We still have the dice box and the little pants, but the draughts board had to be left behind.

One night when we had all dropped off to sleep we were awakened by peculiar stamping and grunting noises. In the dark we lay apprehensively trying to make out the cause of it. At first to our frightened ears the guttural noises sounded like German voices, and the thumping feet like hundreds of men surrounding us. Heavy bodies began to push and bump against the sides of the hut and rattle our insecure door; guessing the cause, George got up to investigate. As he opened the door, several startled reindeer lurched away in fright.

It was a herd of over five hundred which had chosen our hut for a meeting place; finding it hopeless to try to scare so many away, George came back to bed. The melting snow had left a patch of green grass in front of our hut, and the herd pushed and grunted as they jostled each other for it and tried to climb onto our low roof. The leader of the herd had a bell round its neck and with relief we heard the bell tinkling into the distance; but back it would come, and the pushing and snorting started all over again. One reindeer on the roof crashed his whole back leg through the roof – we gazed up fearful that the rest of him would follow, but with a grunt the leg disappeared. After a long two hours or more the reindeer moved on and we settled down to sleep again.

As the days went by, George began to be more engrossed in the problem of our ultimate escape, and at last evolved a plan which we thought might work. One afternoon he decided to try to cross the now rapidly flowing river at its lowest point in order to visit the others in the other valley and discuss his idea with them. At this time the Captain being the senior officer was nominally in charge of affairs, and so out of politeness George had to consult him and Stoddart. Making a bundle of his trousers and boots, and taking a long staff he had made out of a tree, we watched him wade into the freezing water, and with many a plunge up to his thighs, he at last reached the other side. Then he dressed and trudged off in the direction of the hut.

An hour or so later we saw his figure coming down to the river edge again and we ran to be able to meet him when he arrived on our side. This visit established our friendly relations again, and though the plan was more or less approved of, it eventually came to nothing.

As the days wore on, we got to know every tree and fold in the landscape, and many hours we watched it idly, or fearfully, as the case may be. Twice we saw two men and a dog far in the distance crossing the valley and, we thought, making for the direction of our hut. Hastily damping the fire, which we always kept low during the day on account of the smoke (having our hot meal at night), we would shut the door, leave the house and hide in the woods on the hill behind. Then much relieved we would return to our hut again.

All this time German aeroplanes were continuously flying overhead, and when we were caught out of doors and heard the noise of their engines it was our rule to remain frozen until they passed on. We had learned from our airman friend that nothing betrayed people more than looking upwards to the sky. Suddenly upturned faces, he had assured us, were clearly visible; so we would crouch gazing at the ground, hoping our unusual presence in the mountains had not been noticed. Often we thought some of the planes were British, but they always flew high; it was the unmistakable German planes that came low over our heads.

From our position on the hillside we had a good but distant view of the hut we had lived in before, and as the days went by we were struck by the odd behaviour of the four people we had left. Always they came out in couples, and would pace up and down alone, with no sign of the other two. Then they would go indoors and the other two would emerge. Or sometimes all four would be wandering in different directions; we became convinced that they had quarrelled.

One day we saw the Stoddarts coming down to the river, so we too went down to meet them. The river was now so wide and full that it was impossible to cross, but we managed to shout across to each other. Awful rows about one thing and another had resulted in a horrible state of affairs, each couple dividing the food, cooking and eating their own meal separately and not speaking to each other. Both Sylfest and his wife had been up several times to try and smooth things out, but without success. Now the Stoddarts told us that they were going to be moved into another valley. It says much for the discretion of the villagers that they had never mentioned these disgraceful fights to us.

One never to be forgotten day, after many days on our own, the three small boys came up with food and brought out quite casually the awful news that Paris had fallen. We could not believe it, but a day or two later when Sylfest came to see us we learned it was only too true.

As the month of May came to a close, the snow around us melted rapidly and soon we had only bare ground and rough grass on the hills. At midday the sun was warm and we made a short excursion down a sheltered valley, just to see the trees there, already bursting into leaf. The last day of May I heard the cuckoo and remember a pang of homesickness as I leaned against a bare rock, feeling the soft warm air on my face. How indescribably lovely these simple days on the high mountain were! We could all have been utterly happy but for the fear that was always with us.

I remember so vividly this last day of May, because after weeks of tranquility I was suddenly possessed by an unaccountable feeling of unrest and the urge to move on. The day before we had been awakened by the tinkle of sheep bells and had seen a flock of sheep spread over the opposite hills. We knew the Stoddarts were going to move any day, and I could not keep my eyes from their hut, watching for the procession which would be their departure. I suppose I did not want to be left behind; suddenly the valley seemed no longer shut in and safe, but open to advancing summer, and to more unwelcome visitors. Our loneliness made me more anxious. For several days we had had no provisions, and we were down to a diet of fat bacon and beans. We longed for a visitor to bring us news.

The first day of June, after an unaccountably sleepless night, I saw with envy a small procession of people leave the hut laden with belongings, and pass out of sight down the valley.

It was a lovely sunny day, but for once I was blind and deaf to the awakening world around us and I felt unhappy and unsafe in our isolation. Later in the morning we heard the tinkle of more sheep bells and saw another flock of sheep filter over the opposite hillside. This we learned later was the arrival of a shepherd and his wife, who had moved in with the Captain and his wife as they always came up the hills on the first of June.

Sylfest told us that now the better weather was coming, he knew of a hidden valley, which was so inaccessible that even he had not known of its whereabouts until by chance he had stumbled on it.

There he and his friends meant to build us a tiny house, and the sooner it was ready for us the better.

It had been more than a week since we had had a visitor, but that afternoon we saw the three little boys approaching us; we were somewhat disappointed because we longed to know what was going on and the little boys naturally never knew anything. However, they brought us more food and the news that they had been helping with the building of a house for the Stoddarts; the men had been working on it for several days and were nearly finished. As they assured us they were working not very far away, we asked them to take a message to Sylfest to ask him to call and see us on his way home. Within an hour they were back again, with the message for us to pack up our things and follow them to the new valley.

Joyfully, but considerably surprised, we packed up our belongings and cleared up all traces of our sojourn in the place. We had always been careful never to litter the surroundings, and for calls of nature had always gone deep into the woods and carried a spade. The result was that it did not take long to leave everything as we had found it and, each shouldering a large burden, we followed the boys into the valley.

They assured us that it was not far, but we had such heavy loads that we made slow going. George carried an enormous haversack packed with clothes and crockery, with odds and ends dangling from it. I carried, among other things, a pail containing the kettle and food enough for the day. The children helped with the rest, but a large packing case of food had to be left behind.

We scrambled over fields of snow, through low brushwood, over small streams and steep hillsides, until at last we found ourselves high on a mountain peak. Sylfest's eldest son Endre, a boy of thirteen, had led the way valiantly all this time, and now he pointed to a wood far below us where he said the men were busy building the Stoddart's house. The last ten minutes we descended rapidly; there was still snow on this side of the mountains, and we slid down the last steep incline on our seats.

When I reached the bottom, my pail was full of snow collected on the way. We found ourselves in a narrow gulch filled with trees and wild undergrowth, and here built snugly against the cliff we found the new house.

We were greeted warmly by the Stoddarts who had already

spent one night in their half-built hut. Now it was almost complete and they showed us with pride their brand new home. Large rocks had been placed to form three sides of the hut, the cliff-side forming the other. The roof of saplings and turf slanted down almost to the ground, so that the place was quite invisible from a few yards away. A small lean-to at one side made a good storage room. Inside, the men had built a large bed of birch-wood saplings, sturdily supported by large blocks of wood, and now filled with twigs and heather. As yet they had no stove, but a small fire burned on the bare floor, the smoke finding its way out of a hole in the ceiling.

We had a long talk, but mostly we listened to the shortcomings of the Captain and his wife. As we had been, the Stoddarts were so relieved to be on their own again that they were in good spirits and prepared to make the best of their new circumstances.

The men were still busy finishing the house and, as none could be spared, George and Endre and Simon set off again to revisit our hut and bring on the provisions we had left behind. They were gone a long time and when George finally staggered into view, his back bowed under the heavy unwieldy box, we understood why. This second journey and heavy load was just about the last straw for George, and certainly a few weeks before he never could have accomplished a quarter of the distance.

Now we had some coffee and biscuits together, and soon the men began to pick up their axes and belongings, for the job was finished. Then suddenly as we all stood there, there was a terrific roar, and an aeroplane terrified us all by swooping low over our heads. It was so close and so sudden that we all ducked, though in discussion later we hoped that we had not been seen under the low trees.

If we had been observed it would be serious for us, for the Germans would be suspicious of any collection of people building in the mountains. However we could do nothing about it and now our chief concern was to find a roof for our own family for the night. The sun was already low in the sky when Sylfest and his brother-in-law prepared to lead us further over the mountains to another derelict hut they knew of. The only drawback to this hut was that it could be seen from a great distance on all sides, and especially from a rough road which passed near it. We agreed to use it only by night and to leave it early next morning without kindling any fire, but to spend that day in the gorge with the Stoddarts. In only half an hour, we saw our new home and soon we were stuffing the two rough beds with twigs and preparing for the night. We were all so tired that in spite of a slight alarm when a 'rype', a bird the size of a partridge, got stuck in the wide chimney for a few frantic minutes, we all slept the night through.

Next morning we found ourselves almost hidden in a thick white mist, and we quickly stamped into the warmest clothing we had. We had a dry breakfast, as we could not light the fire, and after tidying up and packing a few provisions for the day, we closed the door and set off for the gorge. Our feet and legs were soaked by the time we stumbled on the camouflaged hut again. There was no sign of life, and we did not disturb our sleeping friends, but sat on cold rocks under the dripping trees, and waited for the sun to break through the mist.

At last about eleven o'clock Stoddart emerged greatly surprised to see us and to learn the time. They set about making breakfast and we too built a fire some distance away and had hot coffee and a tin of meatballs and bread. Greatly fortified, we prepared to pass the long day. The mist never lifted, but remained in the valley from dawn to dusk. Our hair was soaked and only by drinking frequent cups of warming tea could we keep ourselves cheerful. The Stoddart's hut looked warm and the height of luxury in comparison with our homeless state and at intervals we went in to warm ourselves.

One of the men from the village came up with things for the Stoddarts and told us that tomorrow they would begin to build *our* house and that we were to wait for them until they came for us. At last the long day ended and we set off again for our sleeping place. Dark was already falling when we finally closed our door for the night, and so with relief we lit a temporary fire and soon, well-fed and comforted, we crept into bed together.

Chapter Seventeen

Next morning we took care to show ourselves very little, except at the back of the hut. When Sylfest, two helpers and his boys appeared we were all ready to accompany them to the hidden valley. We knew we would return that night, so taking only provisions for the day, we fell in behind them, full of anticipation.

The men were laden with axes and saws and we had a fine day for it. Once we passed another derelict hut, and Sylfest hunted through the debris for likely pieces of wood which we carried away with us. There were several great beams lying about, and I shall never forget the casual way Sylfest shouldered one monster onto his back, and to our amazement strode off with it as if it had been made of cork. Later it was to form the important cross-bar of the front of our house.

Over the high hills we followed until at last, crossing a large bog of peat, we could just discern the tree tops of our hidden valley. As we came nearer to it, over difficult ground, we could understand how even these men had never known of its existence. Suddenly we were in the birch trees and enclosed by low hills and thick woods. Entering deep into the trees we came to a spot where several large stones showed where, perhaps hundreds of years ago, a house had stood. Sylfest told us that long ago there must have been a smithy here, for they had found a few bits of ancient iron lying nearby. A smithy in the ageless woods seemed to take us right back to the Norse sagas, and we liked to think later

Building our hut in the birch wood.

that we were living where some forgotten Viking had had his home.

Our house took three days to complete and every day we accompanied the men and helped in any way we could. During the first day the foundations were laid. The three men who were helping us, Sylfest, his brother-in-law and Old Father William, began by collecting suitable large, solid stones, and staggering with them through the birches to the site we had chosen. Soon the rough outline of a house was made and quickly the solid walls began to grow. While this heavy work went on, Sylfest's sons, and Simon and George, felled young straight birches and then stripped the bark from them with knives. These were needed for the roof, and when that was reached, the saplings were spread closely together to form a pointed roof. Meanwhile Old Father William would disappear for long hours, returning with a large bundle of birch bark, cut wholesale and in long curving strips from old trees – without cutting deep enough to kill the tree, he said. Next these were spread over the birch rafters as tiles, until not a chink remained; lastly sods of turf were packed over all.

Our home, in the birch wood. June 2 – June 22

The result was a firm snug roof which could stand up to the severest winter weather. While the roof was being finished Sylfest was busy constructing us four bunks, two above the other, making us rough benches and cupboards out of

---

Here my mother's account ends, interrupted in mid-sentence some day in the 1940s when we were in South America. Repeatedly she sat down to finish it, but as some time had elapsed, she needed to reread the whole manuscript before she could begin again. Unfortunately, re-reading the manuscript came to upset her more and more, and it was never finished. She begged me, Janet, to finish it for her. My mother felt that the finished account would be a tribute to my courageous father and to the brave Norwegian people. I was only a little girl at the time, and though my memory of those days remains very clear, I was not included in the plans and discussions of the adults, so my version will not be as clearly explained. This part of the book was added nearly fifty years later, in 1990.

The building of our hut in the secret wood was an interesting experience. From the materials around us a stout, comfortable and weatherproof home was soon made. The trees that were felled were taken singly far from the hut, and the hut appeared to 'grow' in its surroundings without making any disturbance. We made no clearings and the trees still almost met over the turf roof.

For the first time in months we were to have the luxury of a bed each. Sylfest made us bunks about eight inches deep and then sent us children afield to gather heather. We used sharp camping knives to cut the stems of whole plants as he had shown us. The heather was then tightly packed into the bunks with the roots downwards so that we rested on the buoyant tops of the plants. Then a piece of cloth was spread over the heather and we had soft and comfortable mattresses. After a week or so the mattress became a bit knobbly, but we knew the remedy and a small supply of fresh heather restored our comfort.

We had almost three weeks in this idyllic glade. We were so hidden and unseen that gradually the fears and horrors of our earlier experiences were soon forgotten and I look back on those days as among the happiest of my life. Having been in danger we valued each other in a way that made us very close as a family. It was wonderful for Simon and me to have so much time and leisure to share with our parents.

My father had always been a busy and ambitious man, and apart from early days at the seaside in Spain we had not spent much time in his company. Now we hung on his words and were delighted by his humour and stories. He had always spoken truthfully to us of our danger and his trust had made us loyal and dependable. Both Simon and I were proud of him and proud to be his children. It was out of love that our obedience was instant and that we kept our voices down to a whisper. When things were hard we found his glance of approval made us extra brave.

Simon in particular pulled his weight throughout these adventures. He never needed to be asked to help. He chopped wood, made meals, carried as heavy a load as he could (even secretly removing heavy items from his mother's pack into his own) and was never idle. He encouraged me, and neither of us would have deigned to whimper, cry or complain.

My father had forbidden us to use English when out of doors, to call each other by our names, or to speak above a whisper – not

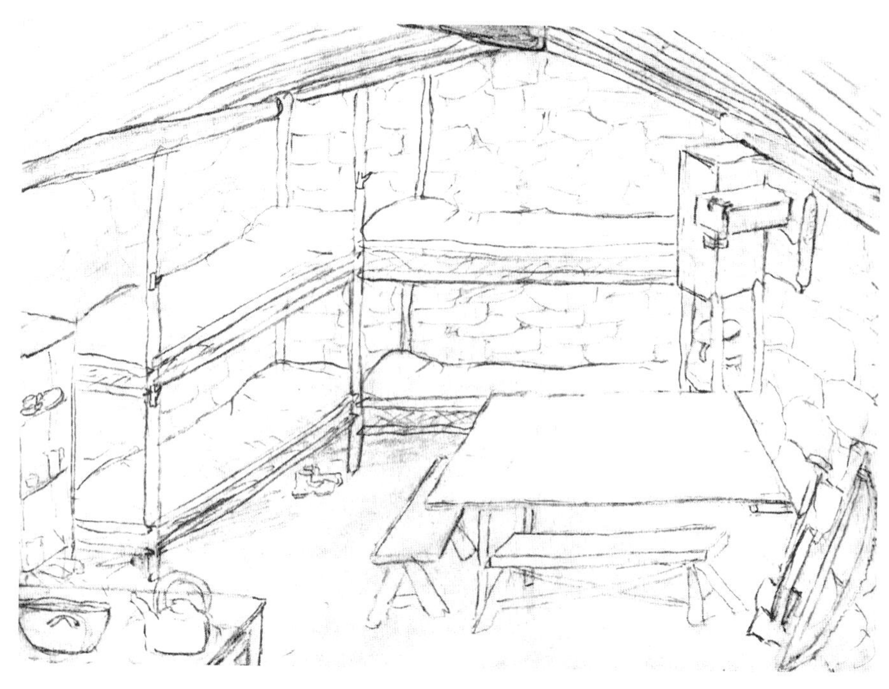

'The luxury of a bed each'.

easy rules for a lively pair of ten- and twelve-year-olds, but we knew how the safety of all of us depended on it and we were eager to prove ourselves.

My mother too, was an inspiration to us. How well she compared with the other women in the group who whined and moaned! It was probably harder for the Russian Mrs. Stoddart, as she was older and unfit – but to us children her tantrums, her cries of 'Henriken! Henriken! What is to happen?', her stealing of food in the night, her spiteful remarks and her rudeness to our noble Norwegian friends, were a revelation. Our mother, by contrast, was quiet and brave and resourceful. We could see how the Norwegian women warmed towards her and how she constantly had to apologise for or to explain away the thoughtless behaviour of the older, rather spoilt, woman.

When we were in the hut in the wood we were away from these irritations. We had time to play in the daytime and my mother would sing us all to sleep at night with her beautiful voice.

Another delight about our hut in the birch wood was that only a few yards from the doorway there was a gully along which ran a sparkling stream. We filled our kettle from a small waterfall and we dammed the stream below to make a bathing pool.

My mother was determined to keep us all clean and in the privacy of the wood, our outer clothes could be washed one day, and our underclothes as soon as the others were dry and ready to wear. Simon and I 'saved' our boots by going barefoot and we spent happy hours by the stream.

Simon has a 'constructive' turn of mind and he soon built a complicated series of working locks in a channel alongside the stream. All these were carefully finished before he diverted the stream of water into them. They worked perfectly and the little model ships my father made for us went smoothly from level to level.

I always admired Simon and what he knew how to do. I thought his locks (remembered from a trip up the Thames) were brilliant. I remember realising that he turned his ship to face mine when it sent a message and that real ships probably didn't, but I wouldn't have mentioned that to him for anything. It made his ship so real and friendly, and the adventures he thought of were wonderful. Unfortunately his wonderful lock system was completely ruined one day when the Norwegian boys came to play with us. They didn't destroy it, but they didn't seem to remember that you could only have one 'parcel' of extra water travelling down through the system at a time. They filled locks at random and soon the banks overflowed and became a muddy morass. Simon smiled and said nothing. I thought he was picturing how the irate Captain would have responded to the destruction of a fortnight's work! Later the muddy banks provided us with hilarious mud baths.

The birch wood around us not only protected us – it was beautiful. There were flowers everywhere and many of the white-barked birch trees were low and twisted, so that they could be 'ridden' like springy horses. In the early morning, when the dew was heavy, I had some favourite cobwebs to visit, some of them almost two feet across, which would be covered in trembling diamonds. In this 'secret' wood they had probably been undisturbed for years. There was time to see beauty . . .

When there was work to be done we all set to at the same time. Kindling had to be gathered and stacked, meals prepared,

Rupert Villiers.

clothes washed, buckets and kettles filled, the oil lamp cleaned and countless other jobs. Then as we finished our tasks, we helped each other, so that we were all free to relax or play at the same time. Fifty years later, I realise how this time shaped our lives. Now when my brother comes to stay in my house I find he will never sit down to read the paper if I am still busy, but will find something helpful to do, and while he washes my car I would feel guilty not to be employed as well. Then with tasks done we can relax together.

In Norway we enjoyed helping and feeling so self-sufficient in the woods. If only we had not needed food! The Norwegians were generous, but we were quite severely rationed. We had one cured ham on a bone, from which my father cut paper-thin slices.

'Playing the violin' he called it – but there was no more hiding of food or arguing about it now we were alone, so it ceased to be a problem.

We grew to know a large ant hill upon which we could throw orange peel or other rubbish and watch it disappear without trace within minutes. It was June and the days were sunny. We gathered sweet whortleberries to eat and we felt Norway was the most beautiful place in the world.

In the evenings my parents used to encourage my teddy to come 'alive'. Although I manipulated him, his compulsive little character became almost real to me. He always asked for explanations which he deliberately misunderstood – he could soon reduce Simon to laughter and even my father spoke to him directly and expected an answer. He was not treated as a toy but as an endearing little companion to us all. There was, however, a brand of Norwegian sardines called 'Teddy' sardines, which troubled him greatly, and if he became too lively or made up one song too many, my father would only need to enquire whether we preferred tomato sauce or olive oil for a certain little bear to decide it was his bed-time!

Those were simple happy days we shared, but they did not last long.

Chapter Eighteen

USUALLY IT WAS THE CHILDREN OF HJØLMO WHO BROUGHT US supplies every three or four days, but in the evenings it would be Sylfest or other men from the village who came to talk with my father. They would sit around the table in the lamplight smoking pipes, while I was supposedly asleep in my top bunk bed. As cigarettes became impossible to get, my father took to smoking a small shiny polished briar that Sylfest gave him. The warm smell of pipe smoke was reassuring to me. It spoke of the presence of strong and thoughtful men.

The Captain had smoked a thinner bitter-smelling tobacco in his pipe when we had been cramped, eight of us, in the first tiny hut. His pipe made a faint squeaking noise as he sucked it. It was this sound which had at first caused his wife to 'hear' footsteps in the snow; of course when he paused to listen, he removed the pipe from his mouth and so we heard nothing. It was Simon who told my father that the alarm was caused by the pipe, and when this was proved to be true we all laughed with relief, even the Captain.

I was afraid of the Captain, he shouted so about little things, but Simon told me I must be sorry for him as he had no teeth and could only eat sops. His wife said that he had left Bergen in such a hurry, that he had forgotten his false teeth which were left in a glass of water. I wondered about this to myself. How could anyone get dressed and go out without their teeth? I wondered whether false teeth took a long time to insert, but then why hadn't he put them in his pocket for later? His short jaw and gummy speech did look odd and I learned to feel sorry for him, but I was still afraid of his short temper. Until that time I had felt that all adults knew best and were to be respected, I had never met any who behaved as our present companions did – so I sat silent, cross-legged in the upper bunk and learned much truth about human nature. I knew, for example, that when my mother gave me half her soup 'because she was not hungry', that she could have eaten four times as much – I accepted it, because that was her decision, but I knew it was done because she cared, and how I loved her for that selflessness.

Now I listened silently as plans were discussed. My father could navigate a boat to England, but the mountain folk did not know the coastal fisher-folk so well – and all fishing boats were monitored by the Germans, compasses had been confiscated and fuel was rationed. There was talk about a submarine coming to fetch us; how thrilled Simon and I were about that, although we were not supposed to know.

One sad night Sylfest brought dreadful news which he told us in a broken whisper – but my hearing is keen – the Germans had come right into a village demanding their stocks of potatoes. They had feared this and had buried more than half their crop in a secret place. They showed the Germans what they had in the barn. The young Germans were not fooled. They both understood and spoke Norwegian. They grabbed a nine-month-old baby from his mother's arms and bayonetted him to the barn door. There he had hung dying before their eyes. The Germans said they would be back for the entire crop of potatoes or the barn door would be 'decorated' again. What could the villagers do? They had fetched their secret supplies, keeping only enough to save themselves from starvation and were awaiting the return visit. The baby was a child of a relation and he choked as he told us what a fine baby it had been – and of the suffering of its mother.

Many Norwegians had suffered from presuming Germans only spoke German. It was ironic that it was the Norwegians' own good will that had caused this extra danger. Apparently, after the First World War, many German children were starving. Fridtjof Nansen the Arctic explorer was a wise politician, and I believe it was he who arranged that through the Red Cross hundreds of German children were brought to stay with Norwegian families and were nursed back to health. These children had learned Norwegian and had later been taught to despise the pity they had been shown.

They had been assigned to the Norwegian invasion forces, but care had been taken that they were sent to a district where they did not know the families. They were in charge now and much of their bestiality and ruthless cruelty towards the Norwegians was in a spirit of distorted revenge and resentment.

Food was short in Germany and planes flew from Norway daily with supplies of food, especially cheese and butter. Sylfest, always gentle and patient with children, had taught us to call the planes '*butter*flies' as they went over – we thought this was witty and enjoyed his 'jokes'. We could smile as we hid from the planes.

I think it was about this time that the Norwegians invented a code name for us. The 'goat's cheese' they called us when speaking to each other, or contacting 'free' Norwegians for plans and information. A chain of contacts was gradually formed right through to the underground movement in Bergen.

At this time my father produced some lists he had written on paper. I am not sure what they were – some of them related to the German production of heavy water in Western Norway, I found out later. To us they were lists of numbers and directions – so many North so many East – quantities and strange place names.

These lists he made Simon and me learn by heart, alternate words to each – after all we were missing school, so it was no hardship. My father would give me a starting word, then Simon and I recited the rest of the list. My words made no sense without Simon's words in between and only my father could start us. When a list was well and truly learned, the paper was solemnly burned. Simon and I knew we were carrying important secret messages for England. After our safe return and my father was to set off for his appointment at the Admiralty, it took him nearly an hour (with our delighted help) for him to make new copies of this secret information.

After the evening visits, when I was lulled to sleep by low voices deep in talk of German activities in Norway, there would be more lists and numbers to be learned the next day.

Chapter Nineteen

On the evening of June 22nd (or early July according to Sylfest when I saw him again six years later, Sylfest, Old Father William and another man came to visit us – but there was no cosy sitting around the table. We were to go, to leave immediately, and as quickly as we could. There was a chance of getting on a boat in a distant fjord. All was arranged, but we must hurry to be there by midday the next day. (I now know that Smä Lars had contacted Wigand Larsen who would have the boat waiting at Erdal, about five kilometres outside Vik in Eidfjord. J. V.) We did not have many possessions, so it did not take us long to pack our rucksacks – but oh how hard it was to leave our safe little world! As we scrambled up the slope out of the valley I stopped for one last look.

'She looks back', said Old Father William with understanding, and his Norwegian phrase also meant 'she remembers'. This kindly man stood beside me where there was the last glimpse of our little home. Then he helped me on, and one of our most exhausting experiences, 'the long walk', had begun.

As we came out of the gully we found the Stoddarts waiting for us. They had been fetched earlier in the evening and had taken rather longer to pack than the Norwegians had hoped. After our friendly greetings we began to march. The Captain and his Swedish wife had elected not to join us. He was increasingly 'unwell' and his wife was determined to get him over the Swedish border to the safety of her own country. I believe she accomplished

Mrs. Stoddart

this eventually, but our Norwegian friends hid and fed them for over a further year.

We were high in the Hardangerfjell and the evening was light. We began by walking down a gully and then we had to remove our boots and socks to wade through an icy river before climbing up a steep mountainside. We followed no visible path, but scrambled over huge boulders until we reached the ridge and then we slid and scrambled down the other side.

Soon we were above tree level through heather, whortleberries and large stone outcrops. We plodded through marshes, squelchy with moss, and then through more shallow icy rivers, and so by midnight we were tired out. It grew dark and we could see clusters of lights down below where there were small villages, but we did not dare go down near to them, for their dogs would bark and give us away.

We had just climbed up a long stretch of rocks when we came to a small path. We followed it upwards through the dark, aware of a

Climbing a stretch of rocks.

steep slope down to our right and the sound of rushing water. The path ended abruptly and from the cliff edge a rope bridge swung out into the dark. We stopped and gathered into a group. The bridge was made of planks knotted together by rope. Some of the planks looked cracked and rotten, and some of them were missing. My father doubted that it was safe.

The Norwegians told us that it was the only way and that we should cross one by one. They suggested that the heaviest should cross last, so that if his weight was too much for the bridge at least the others would be safely over. This meant that the smallest should go first, so I took my place by the bridge. My father told me not to look down and not to worry if the bridge did break, but to cling firmly to it – then I would be able to climb up my piece of it, like a ladder, to either one side or the other. This made sense when I pictured it. Simon offered to go first, but I was already braced for it. I stepped gingerly onto the first planks on which my boots felt very slippery. I held on to the rope hand-rail which was at shoulder height for me; I could not reach across to both handrails together. The planks swayed and so did the rope hand-rail, pulling me sideways. I bent my knees, let go of the hand-rail and proceeded to cross on hands and knees. This felt much safer as I could place my feet more firmly and advance from plank to plank without letting go. The bridge still swung, but not so much with me keeping in the middle.

The first half of the crossing rapidly became more down hill and I could not help glancing down between the planks to see a white frothy river far down below. I gripped firmly, so as to be able to 'climb the ladder', as there appeared no way one could survive a fall into that abyss. Towards the middle, the ladder swung more from side to side – I had to stop once or twice and crouch still until it subsided – then I was climbing upwards.

I had no idea what to expect on the other side, but I had the fright of my life when a large hand grabbed me and lifted me up the last few feet. I was placed beside a tall dark figure in a cape and sou'wester. He just said 'Good' and motioned me to wait away from the edge. Did the others know he was there? Was he catching us? Then he flashed a light into the darkness and there was another flash from the far darkness, and I knew that he must be 'on our side'. The bridge began to creak and heave again so someone else was on their way. The 'guard' knelt down, staring intently along the bridge, one large hand extended to help. Simon came next and then my mother. They had followed my example (as did the rest of the party) and had crossed on hands and knees.

We huddled together against a dark wet rock waiting for my father. Old Father William and the Stoddarts came over. With Sylfest there was ominous cracking of wood, and even more when it was my father's turn. I really thought the bridge would break, but it was not until he was almost with us could I see that it *was* my father who had crossed. Our other Norwegian guide flashed a light and went back the way he had come.

Our new guide then led on at a brisk pace. It was drizzling and we stumbled along behind him. He led us down a hill into a valley and straight towards a small house. The door opened at his knock and we almost fell into a warm bright welcoming room. There were two kind and concerned Norwegian wives there who had prepared a long table of food and coffee for us. They pressed us to have smoked ham (delicious) and cheese and new baked crisp bread. I suddenly found that I was too tired to eat. I thought we had reached a safe place for the night, and I let my head rest on my arms and almost slept at the table. Over my head I could hear the kind lady who carried the coffee pot talking to my mother:

'Leave the little girl here. She will be safe with me. I will treat her as my own daughter. Do not take her into danger – she is exhausted – fetch her when we are rid of the Germans!' I stiffened, instantly awake. I kept my eyes closed to bear my mother's reply – what if I were left!

My mother answered gently, full of gratitude, but she explained that we had come so far together as a family and that she could not bear that we should be parted. She said that I was strong and did not hold them up, which made me proud. Then my father said that I should be roused and given some black coffee with plenty of sugar in it and be ready to go on. As I left the table to gather up my things, that gentle Norwegian lady, who would have risked her life in harbouring an English child, gave me a big hug and a kiss. I returned the kiss, realising that here was a special person, even though I rejoiced in not having to stay.

Then we started again out into the darkness. We walked and walked and walked, not on any proper path, but over the moors and scrambling over the rocks. We seemed to have been well revived by our rest. I felt wide awake again, but my legs felt numb and mechanical. Every now and then we stopped to allow the Stoddarts to catch us up, and I found the re-starting to walk hurt more than keeping on.

We walked until dawn broke, and in spite of drizzle it was beautiful. We sat down for some minutes and had sandwiches and hot coffee from flasks. We gazed around us as we ate. We were high up above tree level in a silent world except for the noise of trickling water from little streams. We had to get down to sea level that day, so we got up and staggered on.

At that stop I had moved over my brother's pack. I was surprised that it was so heavy that I could not lift it. I was only two years younger, but I could not imagine walking so many hours with that on my back! I went over to my mother's pack and I found that I could lift hers. Before I could say anything Simon gave me a look and said,

'Leave it!'

I knew what he had done, but it was not until several years later that my mother learned of the consideration he had shown her.

'He carried me over several rivers'.

We came to a broad river and started to wade across, our boots hanging from our necks by their laces. I found the current too strong and was being swept over when Sylfest caught me. In spite of his knapsack he swung me on to his back and carried me over. He carried me over several rivers after that.

On the far bank we all sat and either put on our boots, or those who had crossed in them took them off to pour out the water. Our socks were already worn into holes, although they were of thick wool, and we all had bright red blisters on our cold white feet. My poor father had a blue toenail from an ill-fitting boot, which was very painful – but his boot had to go back on.

We had been walking almost twelve hours. Had we known we had this long trek ahead of us we would have rested the previous day – but we hadn't known. Simon and my father had been tired from chopping up kindling wood and we had all been nearly ready for bed when the summons had come. Tired is just not the word for how we felt then. No one said a word, but I know I became in a semi-stupor, my limbs burning hot with pain. At every step a beam of pain scorched up each leg and yet I felt far away from it. I found myself dropping back, though I still plodded on mechanically. Suddenly I heard my father's voice beside me, I had not known he was there, as I had ceased to look beyond my next footstep.

'Come on Jan', he said, 'Do this for me, keep going or you know what might happen. Keep on going!'

'Keep on going', I said to myself. I wasn't going to hold anyone up. I stepped out and made sure I wasn't last again. How glad I was when we finally stopped for breakfast.

We built a small fire and had coffee and reindeer sausage. It tasted rather like salami and we ate ravenously. The coffee cleared my head, and though my burning feet felt as though they could explode through my ski-boots, I felt better, and so we went on once more, always heading downhill now, on and on towards the fjord.

We came to another large waterfall and we had to slide and clamber down beside it, finally rock-climbing down foothold by foothold, a great sheer rock. I learned later that there was a two hundred to three hundred metre drop as we did this. At the time I just did not look down, but I knew that a slip meant death.

Then we were going downhill so steeply that we had to hold on to the trees and then drop down towards another tree to prevent ourselves from falling headlong down the hillside. Only once I lost my grip and fell; it seemed to me as if I had landed in a cloud of blackness, but I heard someone say 'keep on going'. I struggled to my feet to find that I had twisted my ankle, but it did not make much difference as I was hurting all over, so that one bit more did not seem to matter. After this slope my father found that he had completely lost his big toenail. He picked the nail off the most horrid blue and red inflamed toe. My mother wrapped something clean around it and then he had to put on his sock and force his poor foot back into his boot. His face went white with pain as he stood up.

'Keep on going', he said and limped on.

We did not stop again for by now we were beginning to fear missing the boat. It was nearly twelve when we saw the fjord shining in front of us. But no, the Norwegians said that there was an impassable river ahead, and that we would have to climb all the way up the mountain on our right and then down the other side.

This was the last straw, but we tackled it, even though it did take an hour.

We arrived at the little village by the fjord and we walked (or tottered) bravely down the street, trying to lift our feet and to look like tourists (very, very weary tourists). Luckily no one seemed to be about at lunch time and we walked straight to the quayside. There was no boat there. We sat on a bench by a wall while Sylfest went off to make enquiries. He came back with the disappointing news that the boat had left about ten minutes before. We had walked for nearly eighteen hours to miss the boat by minutes! Sylfest led us back away from the harbour and the village and hid us in a small wood. Here we just slumped – we were too tired to sleep.

Chapter Twenty

I DO NOT KNOW HOW LONG WE WAITED – I ONLY REMEMBER looking closely at some green leaves and feeling dizzy and sick – it could have been a couple of hours, but I do not remember. I only remember the comfort of that serene plant. Then Sylfest and Old Father William reappeared and led us back to the quayside where a small motor launch was waiting.

It was time to say goodbye to our wonderful and well loved friends from Hjølmo and Øvre Eidfjord. How could we express our thanks? How does one thank those who have saved your life at terrible risk to their own and that of their families? My father shook hands and I watched the men put their free hand on each other's wrists as they shook, emphasising the bond between them. My mother murmured thanks with tears in her eyes and gave Sylfest my thick 'teddy-bear' (artificial fur) overcoat for one of his little girls. I gave and received warm hugs. We boarded the motor boat and were told to hide ourselves below, so there was no waving goodbye. The bravest and finest men we had ever known were suddenly out of our lives.

Larsen and my father were talking. Larsen was slim and lively. He spoke more quickly than our mountain friends and nothing seemed to worry him. He was buoyantly confident and sang at the top of his voice. We who had been quiet and unobtrusive for so long, looked at him in amazement. The trip in the motor boat was not long and soon we were decanted and led into a clean white wooden house overlooking the fjord.

'It was time to day goodbye'.

Our hostess there was most kind and welcoming. She offered us two rooms – a bedroom above and a ground floor sitting room. The Stoddarts elected the upper room. Our hostess plied us with food and blankets, but unfortunately she asked my mother (who was speaking Norwegian and thanking her for everything) whether there was anything else she could get for her mother? Mrs. Stoddart spoke hardly any Norwegian, but she understood the remark, and knew she had been mistaken for my mother's mother. She became quite hysterical, screaming that it was *my* mother who should have been mistaken for the older woman; that she was noted for her youth and beauty, and then came threats to anyone who dared presume that she was anyone's mother! I now realise that she was as exhausted as the rest of us and probably did not know what she was saying. Her husband led her upstairs, still shouting, while he apologised over his shoulder.

Our new Norwegian friend gazed in alarm and my mother tried hard to convince her that Mrs. Stoddart was *not* mad, did not mean what she said, and would be normal in the morning. I had something to eat and some sips of milk and just managed to stagger outside before beginning to vomit.

I found myself in a flower-filled garden and was ashamed to have been sick on the neat flower bed. Our new hostess told me it was nothing and carried me indoors – I was placed on a sofa in the sitting room and tucked up with rugs, with a reassuring bowl beside me. It was utter exhaustion and for two days I lay there being sick. On the third day I was allowed to sit in the sun in the beautiful garden (all signs of my disgrace were gone).

My body was stiff and aching and I could hardly walk. I hadn't the strength to chew, but our gentle hostess brought me frequent sips of broth and I slowly recovered. How caring she was and how brave. As we had walked into Erdal we had seen Nazi posters that listed my father's name. It made clear that helping any English would mean a death sentence. Even so this courageous lady made us feel wanted and cared for.

My father had studied the poster and was pleased to see the names of others he knew who had also presumably eluded the Germans. Best of all, he said, was that the poster showed the Germans were looking for *men* on the run, and had no idea that women and children were involved. He said we were his best disguise.

The Stoddarts came down from their room in the day and sat in our warmer sitting room. My father was explaining plans to Mr. Stoddart while his wife refused to speak to us. She sat playing patience, coming out with odd remarks like,

'I have always been *noted* for my beauty!' to the room in general.

Nobody replied, as we had learned that anything said while she was in one of these moods would lead to a magnificent outburst of Russian 'nerves'. Her 'nerves' we had been told, were a sign of her good breeding and that she, in common with other White Russian nobles, was sensitive to phases of the moon.

'In Moscow on a moonlit night, the roof tops are crowded with people of passion!' she had once said. We imagined some strange scenes! In later years when we met anyone whose behaviour appeared odd, we would murmur to each other

'In Moscow on a moonlit night!'

My father spent many hours with maps at the sitting room table, talking with Larsen and other men who came and went. He

The potato hut on Syltøy island.

was sometimes away with them for some hours, which made my mother anxious. I think we were about three days in that hiding place and then we were hurried out to a motor launch again. We seemed to be leaving the mainland coast and headed out between rocky deserted islands.

We disembarked at a landing stage and from there we walked up a valley path. At first there was no sign of human habitation, but we finally came to a house which had an outlook out to sea, but we appeared to have approached by some back way. Here we were welcomed and given a meal – lovely creamy white fish balls in a white sauce. 'Stavanger eggs' I think they were called. Then we were led across the island again (about a quarter of an hour's walk) to a remote 'potato hut' overlooking the fjord. It was a small two-storied building used for storing potatoes; there was a table and benches and an iron stove in the downstairs room and we slept on the floor amongst the few sacks of potatoes in the upper room.

My father then told us about the boat in which we might cross to England and which he had first heard about from Smä Lars. We had travelled all the way down from the High Fjell just for this chance. He explained that there was an American who lived in Bergen who had an English wife and two little daughters. As America was still a neutral country at the time, he had not been arrested, but he was on a sort of parole. He had to report in person to the Germans every morning and evening. This American had somehow obtained a 'launch' or yacht and was secretly fitting it up. He wanted to get his English wife to safety, as frightening things were happening. He knew my father could navigate and he invited our party to join him. My father would not agree until he had seen the boat and disappeared for the whole day with Larsen.

The little rocky bay around the potato hut was an idyllic place to be. Simon and I have always loved water and the sea, and now we spent hours quietly exploring rock pools. The rock pools were beautiful; each a little world of its own. I chose one as my favourite and then searched other pools for brightly coloured seaweeds and coloured stones. All the other 'treasures' were transferred to 'my pool'. Most of the different seaweeds were clinging to stones so they could be moved without killing or picking them. My pool became the most beautiful garden and after each high tide I would return to it to see which small fish or shrimps had moved in to enjoy it.

When I mentioned the shrimps to my mother, Mrs. Stoddart overheard me and asked why I couldn't do something useful like catching shrimps for us to eat? I thought I'd try and I took a tin mug down to the rock pools. Any shrimps that were in my pool were safe. That pool was special and should remain a fishy haven. I found that although I had no net, I could catch shrimps between two handfuls of seaweed. It was beginning to get dark when I returned to the potato hut – my tin mug was over half full, I think I caught twenty-three shrimps and was pleased to present my catch to be cooked.

'What's the use of only a few shrimps each?' complained Mrs. Stoddart. We each had our share on a piece of potato bread including the Stoddarts. It *did* look rather meagre and so I did not go shrimping again. I would rather see them darting happily in their pools!

That evening my father returned with bad news. He had seen the launch and he said that under no circumstances would he risk our lives in such a flimsy vessel. It was big enough, he said, but it was a pleasure boat, built for sheltered waters. He said people did not realise the power of the North Sea and it was out of the question. My father had done his utmost to dissuade the American from making the attempt, but had not succeeded. He told me the little girls each had a Shirley Temple doll, just like mine in England. He thought he could arrange it for me to take my teddy and go over to play with them one day. I looked forward to that.

The next day Larsen came up the fjord, singing at the top of his voice. This alarmed my father, but Larsen said that if he pretended to be drunk the Germans just laughed at him and did not search him. He then produced two quite large parcels for the Stoddarts. Apparently they had paid him most of their remaining money to go to their flat in Bergen and to collect some of their treasured possessions – particularly a Russian icon. My father was appalled at the risk that he had taken, as Larsen could easily have been followed or identified. Most of all my father was displeased that this had all been arranged behind his back. Larsen was amused and said he had spoken to Germans who did not suspect him. He then proceeded to 'entertain' us by showing us how he could swallow raw eggs! Indeed he could, and he consumed most of our meagre supply – just breaking them into his mouth and gulping them down, without another thought!

My father went to the owner of the potato hut and with his help and contact with a Bergen resistance leader, Henrik Platou, it was finally arranged that we could hire a fishing boat. Our host was taking a risk, as all the boats were registered with the Germans and its disappearance would have to be explained. He did not hesitate. Time and time again we were left amazed at the courage and loyalty of the Norwegians. They did not question as to whether to resist the Germans and take risks – we never once met one who was not a patriot, thoroughly anti-German and ready to help us. Airmen landing in France could never know whether the people at the nearest farm would not sell them to the Germans – but the country people of Norway were dependable. It is a pity that their one traitor, Quisling, should give his name to treachery. Norway should not be remembered for Quisling.

Then came bad news. The American had been arrested as he set off in his boat. Apparently he was being 'watched'. We were told that his wife and the two little girls had been shot. The Norwegians could not get over the murder of the children. I believe they were about six and eight years old. The soldiers had taken the Shirley Temple dolls – would they think of the children they had killed as they gave the dolls to their own children? Perhaps they just stole them to sell.

* * *

After this news I sought the refuge of the beautiful world by the rocky shore. I sat by my 'special pool' and had time to think. I looked at the beauty around me and wondered why some humans fought and killed like savage animals let loose in paradise. I was not afraid. I had not been afraid in our adventures after meeting the young airman Farragut. A conversation with him had changed my whole concept of life and its purpose.

My mother has told of the events of the most frightening day that led up to our stay in Odda. In my mind I have always called it 'The Worst Day'. It was when we woke to gunfire in that bright farmhouse at the cross-roads. There was glass everywhere from the shattered windows and bullets were pitting the walls like vicious wasps. As we got dressed, lying under the beds to avoid the bullets, I was afraid. Simon was not at all ruffled. When we went down the stairs towards the cellar, a bullet missed his head by inches. He drew out his pocket knife and tried to remove the bullet from the wall. When he was told to keep down, he justified his action quite calmly saying,

'That bullet almost killed me.' He didn't get it though.

Then when we were in the cellar, with the fighting all around the house it was incredibly noisy and frightening. In films soldiers seem to fight silently, but these men were shouting orders, some in Norwegian some in German – injured men were shouting, shots were everywhere and all was noise and confusion.

We were sitting with our backs against a bricked-in doorway, so immediately outside our wall there were stairs down to an ideal hiding place for a sniper. We heard someone clatter down the steps in heavy boots and we heard him grunt as he loaded his gun – his shots were loud, but suddenly he gave an even louder scream and we heard him slump down. We did not know whether he was German or Norwegian, but even if he had been German we could only pity his agony. The fighting around the house was so intense no-one could have ventured out to help him, so with only a few bricks between us, we listened to him die. Again it was not like the films; he screamed and gasped and groaned – one could hear the blood choking his throat – it was terrifying to hear, and then he gurgled, made strange throat noises and died. It all took too long.

Then the German came into the cellar. My father was hiding in a potato sack by then. The German shouted 'Hände hoch!' Our Norwegian hostess spoke to him. He had a bayonet and I could imagine it being thrust through the potato sacks where my father was hidden. Yes, I was afraid. Then as we left that house, the garden was littered with bodies.

'Hold my hand and don't look', my mother said. I obeyed, but I had already seen the piles of bloody clothes which had once been men.

Worst of all was the last bus ride that day, when my mother describes me as singing so cheerfully. My parents had been given seats near the front of the bus, but there was no seat for me, so I had been sent down towards the back. A big man reached out and placed me to sit on his knee that was jutting out into the aisle. The soldiers around me had been fighting, they were exhausted and they smelt of blood and sweat. Some of them were wounded and groaning with their heads back. All of them seemed to have pale green faces with sweat on their upper lips.

The bus went at break-neck speed, as if it wanted to crash into the grey cliffs, only swerving violently at the last moment. We drove without lights to avoid being seen, and the bus hurtled faster and faster into the dark. Across the aisle a man was muttering a prayer over and over again.

'I have a little girl your age', the giant holding me muttered. 'When will I see her again? Do you go to school? Can you sing a hymn?' he demanded. It was not *my* idea to sing! I sang 'God is good', the hymn I had sung so happily in Nygaard Skole in Bergen. When I finished, several voices said,

'Again, again', so I sang it again.

My fear gathered as the night grew blacker and the bus went faster, and the men around me were so desperate for any distraction.

The bus was going to plunge into an abyss or the Germans were going to shoot us – we were all going to die I knew for certain.

'Sing again, sing, sing', came from all sides.

So with a strange despair in my heart I kept on singing – I was afraid, but the men around me were afraid – I had not realised that grownups could be afraid. I realised that everyone in the world has to face death alone – I sang and my childhood's ideas dropped from me like losing a protective coat. I was going to die – so that's what life was about! 'God is good!' I sang yet again, but my heart cried out,

'If God is good, I don't understand!'

The next day, though we were now in a civilized house and I had had a warm bath, I was still shaking – the world did not appear to be real any more. Humans were only play-acting in the face of death.

After lunch when Farragut had entertained us with his stories, Simon and I were left alone with him. Simon still remembers how he described his 'Swordfish' seaplane, that flew so slowly, he said, that the German guns automatically fired in front of him, as the sightings on their guns were geared for faster aircraft. He had told us about a torpedo he carried between his two landing floats and the three home-made bombs he carried to either side of him. There was a small trap door in the floor, between his knees and he could drop his home-made bombs down on the German installations with great accuracy! He was as gallant as a knight in armour.

'But aren't you afraid?' I asked. He put his arm around me as he replied, and I can feel the warm leather jacket he wore even now.

'Afraid of what?' he asked.

'To die', I said. He looked kindly at me and said,

'I hear you had a pretty bad time yesterday.'

Then he went on to explain that he was not afraid to die, because he knew he was doing right. Only people who had bad consciences need wake with nightmares in the night or be afraid to die. We all had a life to live, he explained, and then we would die; sooner or later did not matter, the thing was to die with a clear conscience. He knew he was risking his life, but if he flew off back to England and did not try to help to get the Germans out of Norway he would be a coward. He could not bear to live as a coward. What would his life be worth if he had that to look back on? He made death sound the natural end to an interesting experience, supervised by a kindly God. He had a strong Christian faith.

'Do what is right', he said, 'and you will never fear anything, even death.'

I understood it all, and my fear vanished. I loved this fine man who had troubled to explain things to a little girl. I felt quite brave and different as I turned back to resume the adventure of life. I cannot remember every word he said, but being comforted by him gave me a strong faith. My faith has developed over the years, but it was he who made it clear to me, set me a goal and made me fearless. Later we heard that his plane had been shot down.

'Nothing remained', the Norwegians said, but my brother and I knew that something would always remain, the memory of that brave man.

Chapter Twenty-one

It was arranged that we should leave in the fishing boat one evening soon. It was the date of the German Commandant's birthday and great celebrations were planned. The coastal air patrols were at least every hour, but we hoped that on that night the patrols might have been drinking and be less vigilant, or might be in a hurry to return to the celebrations. At that time of year there was little chance of not being seen, so we hoped to be overlooked or ignored.

The fishing boat was a sturdy fifty foot long diesel-powered North Sea vessel. It later made several return trips to Norway carrying free Norwegians for resistance work. We were told some Norwegian boys, hoping to join the free Norwegian navy in England, would be hiding in the hold. All sea charts had been confiscated by the Germans, but luckily Simon had a small compass from a Christmas cracker. With that tiny compass and the bearings from a land map, my father worked out our route.

At dusk the Norwegian who owned the potato hut came to see us off. We got into the rowing boat to go to where the fishing boat was hidden. The Norwegians gave us some food supplies – reindeer sausage and crispbread made from some petrol-contaminated flour the Germans had dumped. Then our Norwegian friend produced the most enormous lobster.

'Take this for King Haakon', he said. 'Tell him it is a token that his loyal subjects are thinking of him and will rejoice at his safe return.'

We got in to the rowing boat.

That lobster *was* flown to King Haakon as soon as we landed, and his message of thanks was broadcast by the BBC. Our friends heard it and then knew we had reached England safely and this was also confirmed by the coded message,

'A cargo of gjeitost (goat's cheese) has arrived.'

As we loaded our supplies on board our Norwegian friends bowed their heads and said the Lord's Prayer. My father then bowed his head and led us all in the Lord's Prayer in English. It was all suddenly solemn and dignified. Our good friends waved to us as my father took the oars and rowed us into the night.

We rounded a rocky headland and there was the fishing boat waiting in the clear moonlight. We climbed aboard and my father made us go below straight away into a tiny two-berthed fore cabin. He said voices would echo over the quiet fjord waters at night, so

We climbed aboard the 'Sjøglimt'.

we could only whisper in the cabin and not speak at all on deck. We heard another rowing boat arrive with the Stoddarts, who were shown to a rear cabin. My father and Simon went to the wheelhouse on deck and were shown the controls. The engine started to throb with a loud 'chunkety-chunk' noise that seemed to shout through the night. The Norwegians climbed down into the rowing boats, and we were off.

My mother and I crept out of our stuffy cabin and onto the deck. The tall grey walls of the fjord were sliding past us. Everything was moonlit and gleaming. Our little boat seemed to be weaving in between small islands. We could see bright stars in the clear sky and we knew that any plane would see the boat easily against the shining water. It grew rougher as we neared the open sea. As the boat rounded from an island we entered a thick mist. It grew chilly, there was no longer anything to see – only the mist veiling the grey open sea ahead, so my mother and I went back into the warm cabin. Neither of us have ever been good sailors so we lay down on the bunks, the better to bear the increasing swell as the boat forged ahead.

Suddenly the engines cut out. There was complete silence, only the slap of the waves against the side of the boat. For a minute or two we wondered whether it had broken down and then we heard the distant engine of an aeroplane. Our boat rolled from side to side, seeming to be almost splashing in the water, as the aeroplane grew louder and passed close overhead. My father appeared in the companion way. He told us the patrol plane had just passed over us. Luckily for us the mist was still so thick that he hadn't been able to see it, so it could not have seen us. Then he went back and restarted the engine and we headed out to sea once more.

It grew more and more rough. We were being tossed about in our bunks, not only from side to side, but up and down as well. I had to lie face down and hold on to the edges of my bunk to prevent being thrown out. Soon both my mother and I were painfully seasick – sharing a bucket between us.

Simon was sent down by my father to get some rest, but the smell in our cabin was too much for him and he returned to the wheelhouse – luckily he has always been a 'good sailor' like his father. He spent the whole night in the wheelhouse, and steered the boat alone for about three hours to give his father a rest. That was quite a responsibility for a young boy, but he was always steady and reliable.

The next day we met a real storm. The cabin seemed to be going up and down like a lift. My mother and I had both been so sick that there was nothing left in us. We held on to our bunks, writhing with the pain of our empty stomachs being wrung by seasickness. I felt so awful that I had no idea of the passage of time and gazed in a stupor as our belongings were thrown from one side of the cabin to the other. Simon was with my father in the wheelhouse. He told me that the seas were so great that the little ship was making no headway. She had been making a steady 5 knots, but when the storm hit her, each wave turned her 15 degrees off course, and it was all they could do to keep turning her into the waves so that she could ride them. All that day my father and Simon battled through the storm. They ate cold 'Stavanger eggs', fish balls out of a tin, and held on to the wheel as the waves crashed over the deck. Simon says he thought it would never stop.

By evening the storm lessened and the boat was able to go forwards again. There was a compass on board but my father had been told it had not been 'corrected' for some years. Simon had a small pocket compass and they compared the two and headed south-west. There was no way my father could be sure how much we had drifted in the storm. Simon says he was using 'dead reckoning' and other instruments of calculation, but they were both so tired that they took turns to sleep or take the wheel the whole time.

Occasionally the next day my father looked in to the cabin and persuaded us to drink water, but my mother and I felt too ill to move. The Stoddarts had also been too ill to move during the storm, nor had there been any sign of the Norwegian boys, so all the navigation had depended on my father and his now thirteen-year-old son.

On the third morning we were still chugging across the sea. The movement was surging, but not as rough as before. My mother and I emerged shakily for a breath of air. It was bright and clear and there was nothing but a vast expanse of sea around us. The fishing boat felt very small. On the deck was the 'important sack'. It contained our passports and secret papers my father had collected. On our journey the 'important sack' had been buried, some distance away from where we were staying each night, and was only dug up when we moved on. Now it sat against the side, with a heavy stone added to its contents, ready to be thrown overboard at the first sign of trouble.

Simon made some coffee and plied us all with reindeer sausage and 'petrol bread'. We all felt better, but we scanned the sky for planes all the time. The Stoddarts and the Norwegian boys did not emerge, but we knew they had food supplies of their own. My father checked that they were all right, while Simon took over the wheel. My father was so proud of his son and the responsibility he could take, it was plain to see.

It was in the afternoon that we heard another plane. It was coming towards us and there was no hiding from it, so my father kept the engine going. We listened intently to the approaching plane.

'It's English!' Simon said. 'It has an English engine!'

He was right. We could hear the steady drone of an English plane. The German planes had different sounding engines that varied in tone as if they were rowing through the air in surges. As it drew near, Simon identified it as a Sunderland flying boat. It came closer and began to circle around us. We waved exultantly.

We did not know that the Germans had been using Norwegian

fishing boats like ours, as decoys. Then as the English patrol planes drew near to investigate, hidden guns would be uncovered and the Sunderlands would be blasted out of the air. The approaching plane had its guns aimed at us and it did not come too close. It circled around us again.

Of course we were delighted to see them. We continued waving cheerfully. I held my teddy bear up high so that he too could wave at the plane and share our relief. It was a little girl holding up a blonde Rupert Bear-style teddy, (he was about twenty inches tall) that made them decide to take photographs instead of firing. (Years later I met someone in Intelligence who had seen the photograph and she told me that my teddy had been identified as a Rupert Bear as sold in Bentalls in Kingston, and from that they had been almost sure that we were the Villiers family who had been listed as 'Missing in Norway'.) German teddy bears were brown, with small eyes and pointed noses. English Rupert bears were quite different, and this was clearly an English toy. To our dismay the plane just left us. My father thought of encouraging remarks –

'They've gone to prepare a welcome for us', he said, but the plane had not stayed long enough to notice the semaphore signal he had begun.

It must have been a couple of hours later that another plane appeared, approaching from England. It dropped a large yellow bundle into the sea near to us and headed away. This plane came much closer and we could see a cheerful face and a waving hand before it departed. It was quite difficult to retrieve the life-belt from the sea. My father manoeuvred the boat as near as he could and stopped the engine, but the bobbing life-belt drifted sharply to port. It took some time before we were near enough to be able to throw a rope at it and lash it towards us. It was a long stretch for my father to get it up on the deck. It was a life-jacket and there was a message in a container.

Mr. Stoddart had come up on deck to see why we were stopping and starting. My father told him that the message said that there was a minefield ahead and that we should alter our course. Best of all the message gave us our exact position. My father was surprised to learn we were much further north than he had supposed and that we were approaching the Shetland Islands. If we had not been seen we might easily have found ourselves heading across the

Atlantic! With a limited supply of water on board and now only a little reindeer sausage and petrol bread left (we would not count the Royal Lobster) we were definitely not equipped to cross the Atlantic.

Simon and Mr. Stoddart watched out for mines as we changed to a more northerly course. Simon told me that a wooden fishing boat could not attract magnetic mines and our draught was so shallow that we would be able to see any mines that might threaten us. This was good news.

With what joy we saw land ahead! Still chugging loudly we entered the port of Lerwick. A small motor launch came out to us and a man with a megaphone shouted instructions. The harbour was so crowded with ships that there was no room at the quayside. We had to tie up against a frigate. While my father was mooring the boat, my mother had gathered all our things. By the time we tied up we were ready to go. My father picked up the 'important sack' and his knapsack and led the way. We crossed the frigate with our noisy ski boots clattering on the metal decks and we were a bit dismayed at seeing that sailors on the quayside had rifles pointing at us as we disembarked. There was a naval officer coming around a warehouse who stared at my father and called out,

'Good God! It's George Villiers! What the hell are you dressed like that for?'

My father *did* look odd in his patterned Norwegian jersey, tartan shirt, plus fours and heavy boots! This welcome was music to his ears, as the rifles were lowered and he shook hands with a fellow naval officer from his Dartmouth days.

There were a few moments to wait. The seagulls screamed a welcome over the quayside while my father explained about the Norwegian boys and saw them safely led off to some naval Headquarters.

We were led through narrow streets to a hotel, to begin the preparations to return to civilized life as my mother has described in the opening chapter.

Afterword

A FEW THINGS REMAIN TO BE SAID. FIVE OF THE GALLANT MEN who had risked so much were awarded the George Medal. The Norwegian Embassy in London has told me that they were:

Sylfest A Myklatun
Lars L. Saebø
Lars K. Myklatun
Svein Kleivkäs
Sjur Hjømo.

My father had the pleasure of being stopped by the armed guards outside the Admiralty when he took them all his information. It was he who told them about the heavy-water plant in Western Norway which would have allowed Germany to develop an atom bomb. He had maps showing its precise location and he was immensely gratified to learn later how promptly it had been destroyed.

We also had some plans which had been stolen from the Germans, of an invasion of England approaching from right round Scotland and invading Liverpool. This too was foiled by the laying of minefields. I do not know what else was in the 'important sack' or what was meant by the lists Simon and I carried in our heads.

There was only one difficulty my father encountered at the Admiralty. When he told them of the mist that had shielded us from the German patrol plane, they looked at him in disbelief. It had been a fine clear July night they insisted. They even checked with the British patrols. Officially there was no mist that night – but we all saw it and it saved us.

My father was rewarded by being taken out of relatively active service and he was posted to Buenos Aires and Montevideo as the officer in charge of all visiting British shipping. He supervised the installation of anti-mine degaussing systems into ships and was called out at night for fires and other emergencies and when merchant and naval ships came in for repairs. He was later promoted to Commander RN.

We sailed out to South America in the liner *Highland Brigade* after only a couple of weeks in London. Simon and I were sworn not to mention Norway for the sake of those who had helped us. Only one thing nearly gave us away. When Simon went into the swimming pool, he was so muscular, lean and brown compared with the pallid English boys! People stared at him and I do not know how my father explained it. It was hard not to say anything about what we had been through, but keeping it secret was another achievement well within our ability. So, strengthened by our experiences we sailed to a new life.

After the war we had the opportunity to return to Norway and to thank our many wonderful friends. They had all survived and they gave us the most moving celebrations that I shall never forget.

* * *

We not only owe our lives to the fine folk of Norway, but by their example we have learned of the courage, honour and dignity to which mankind should aspire.

Letter to Commander George Villiers RN (Retd.)

A letter from Smä Lars in 1946 in answer to my father. My father's report led to the award of five George Medals shortly after this.

Eidfjord Gjestgjever
January 8, 1946

Dear Sir!
I congratulate you with the peace and victory! and we are very glad to hear you all well and living. I received your letter a few days before Christmass and believe me we was very thankfull to you for giving us such a glad message. It came as a great Christmas gift.

To know that the war is over – all you that was here still living – and also we – your friends – the same, certainly is a great pleasure and gives a lot of good feeling; and we hope and expect to have the pleasure to see you all here again and shake hands. We are looking forward to that *great glad* day. Certainly we had a great time in the country from one end to the other, now when the English and Americans was here and disarmed the Germans – I believe that those that had the job was very satisfied with it!

Well, we got rid of the bad parasites we had been feeding in all those five years. Wonderful thing! Those rascals robbed the country for everything from one end to the other, and every little community had to sell a lot of the crop for a small pay to the dirty invaders.

I may tell you that we here in Eidfjord have not been starving during the war, but have had our living as usually.

Certainly we was in want of different things such as fine flour, coffee, sugar, then more. It was very difficult to get any shoes and clothing, so we had to wear our old 'rags' – and are still doing it! But we should worry!!

Now when we are a free people – not robbed of anybody – everything that we need will be coming our way little by little, so from last fall things has changed a great deal.

Your are telling me that you have reported about me and Sylfest what we did and risked for you. Well, I may tell you that I did not do any more than my simple duty so that is nothing to mention. We did not do much – and did not dare to do any more on account of the risk for all of us. I feel sure that the Germans never got to know anything about you – good thing they did not – a lucky thing for us here!

For your deep gratitude and admiration we are very thankfull.

With very best regards to all of you we wish you a happy New Year!

Yours most sincerely,
Lars L. Saebø

A copy of the report made by our Eidfjord friends which was sent to England in August 1946

Two British gentlemen – 2 ladies and 2 children arrived at Hjølmo farm from Mr. LARS. L SAEBØ, Øvre Eidfjord in April 1940 and they stayed at Hjølmo farm proprietor Lars K. Myklathun 6 days. As they were short of money a message was sent to the neighbourhouse to Mr. SYLFEST A. Myklathun, and he was asked to go to Ustaoset, Bergens railway to Oslo with a letter to Mr. St. John, the vice consul from Bergen, who they suggest was there. Mr. Sylfest agreed and went to Ustaoset with two letters, the one for the Director Cappelen at Ustaoset Hotel and the other to Mr. St. John. He went first up to the Director Cappelen and after he has seen over the letter and burnt it, he was put on the way to the hut where Mr. St. John and wife was hiding. Mr. St. John made an investigation to obtain money, but it was impossible as all the cash had been brought in safe because the germens was on their way along the railway truck. The Germens was allready on Geilo St.

After a while Mr. St. John asked Mr. Sylfest about the Germans in Eidfjord how many it was there, but they was not arrived there at the moment. He asked therefore Mr. Sylfest to come with him to Eidfjord as he thought it was safer there as along the railway line. Mr. St. John and wife (Norw. born) followed him over the Hardanger mountains on ski to Storeli leitet, and here from to Lars Garen and they ended at Mr. Lars Liseth just near Fossil Hotel for the night. This place was to close for the main road, and they were therefor sent away to Øvre Eidfjord, where the shopkeeper Ola Myklathun shoved them the way to Hjølmo far the same day. The first night at Hjølmo farm the Germens arrived at Eidfjord. Messrs. Sjur S. Hjølmo and John J. Viverlid helped them with the transport. After the arrival of the germens a stream of fugitives went up the Hj\o lmo valley and it was necessary to have the British people up in some dairy huts opposit Hjolmo. As it was very uncomfortable and a small place, Mr. Sylfest took 4 of them over to Kjukkaskog hut and Mr. Sjur S. Hjolmo helped with the transport to this place. To get them better hidden it was decided with assistance with Mr. Sjur S. Hjolmo and Brigt Burkeland to build 2 stone huts, where Mr. and Mrs. Villiers with 2 children could stay in this one and in the other Mr. and Mrs. Studdard in The other. This was done.

To Mr. and Mrs. St. John Mr. Lars. S. Viverlid built a stone hut on the top near Valurwaterfall, but as son as the families Villiers & Suddard departed in July, Mr. & Mrs. St. John mooved to the hut of Mr. Studdard. Mr. St. John counted the days he stood here to 99 days, when they mooved to Mr. Gunnar E. Viverlid (Touriststation hut) late in the autumn, and where Mr. Lars. S. Viverlid saw to them. By Gunnar E. Viverlid the stayed to the new year and mooved up to Mr. Lars S. Viverlid and stayed here 4 weeks and mooved back again to Mr. Gunnar E. Viverlid in the new year 1941. In the Easter days 1941 Mr. Gunnar E. Viverlid waited guests for the holidays and he was afraid to have them there, where as they was mooved down to Djupskjelle outfarm (hut).

Mr. Sylfest A. Myklathun was engaged in the transport of food to his brothers but Rauhelleren Touriststation, this easter hollidays, and after a conference with his brother Hans A. Myklathun they decided to give Mr. Magister Somme, who was on the Rauhelleren this easter, information about the 2 british difficulties staying at Hjolmo. Mr. Magister Somme was at once preparede to help and said that he within 3 weeks should come to Djupskjel hut and clear up all for transport away from this place. At the promised time Mr. Somme arrived at the home of Mr. Sylfest A. Myklathun and was followed up to the stonhut. There they cleared up the plan for the flight to Schwede. Then Mr. Hans A. Myklathun should wait for a letter from Mr. Somme, containing letters or papers to Mr. & Mrs. St. John, and atonce follow the party to Rauhelleren. Just over Easter the letter arrived and Mr. Hans A. and Sylfest A. Myklathun followed them to Rauhelleren, where they arrived a saturaday evning, and early Sunday mornin at 6 ocklock arrived Mr. Somme. Then Mr. Somme took over for the further transport.

The departure from the stonhuts with the Villiers & Studdard families took place in July 1940. A message fr Mr. Lars L. Saebø, Ø. Eidfjord told them to come to Erdal 5 km outside Vik, Eidfjord at 12 oclock next day. Here a motorboat was ready to transport and a man from Bergen (Mr. Wigand Larsen) as leader. They who followed these families on all 6 prs. were Sylfest A. Myklathun, Lars S. Viverlid and Brigt Byrkeland. The departed from the stonhuts about 9 oclock p.m. and stopped at Lars S. Viverlid for food 3 hours, and went away again at 12. ni to pas over the mountains for Erdal. They went over the mountains in a rainy and ruff weather and in the dark ni to the Erdal dairy hut, on the edge of the mauntain to begin on the track down to Erdal. This was the most difficulty part of the track, as they on one of the track parts had to hold fast to a wire to come over the slops. In the plain ston wall there wer some cuts for the feet, and more than 2–300 meters canyon below. it was a little brighter now in the morning and they got the order not to look down in the canyon – only fix the eyes to the rocks, then it would be all right.

The leader wer afraid that the shildren and women should feel dizzy, but all went after plane and they arrived at 12 oclock in Erdal. But no motor boat was on the place. They arrived safely and unseen down to shore and took place hidden in a birckwood. Soon after 1 oclock the motorboat with Mr. Wigand Larsen arrived. The Viverlid depated from the Britishi in the wood and the families quickly boarded the motorboat, and there were only some youths and people from Erdal on the quay.

This Report is taken up in Eidfjord 14 August 1946 and signed by.

Sylfest A. Myklathun
Lars L. Saebø
Lars S. Viverlid
Ola Myklathun
Hans A. Myklathun
Gunnar E. Viverlid.

Telefon 11283
Telegramadresse: PLATOCO

Girokonto:
Bergens Privatbank, nr. 23145

H. PLATOU & CO. A/s

Resident Representative of
Raleigh Industries Ltd. Nottingham (Engl.)

Incorporating:

THE RALEIGH CYCLE CO LTD.
RUDGE WITHWORTH LTD.
HUMBER LTD. (CYCLE DEPT.)

THE ROBIN HOOD CYCLE CO. LTD.
STURMEY-ARCHER GEARS LTD.
THE NOTTINGHAM PRESSWORK LTD.

BERGEN, 3rd August, 1948.

Commander George Villiers,
Simmington,
Yorkshire,
England.

Dear Mr. Villiers,

I want to express my heartfelt thanks for your visit, I was so pleased to get a glimpse of those whom I did my best to help to get over to England again. From our short conversation you will have understood that also I was equally happy to see that everything went well.

I highly appreciated your visit, which meant much more to me than any official reward.

With my best wishes to your wife and daughter,

Yours sincerely,

H. Platou.
Henrik Platou.

I enclose 3 copies of the report I took up in 1946.

By the KING'S Order the name of
Sylfest A. Myklathun,
was placed on record on
10 June, 1947.
as commended for brave conduct.
I am charged to express His Majesty's
high appreciation of the service rendered.

C. R. Attlee

Prime Minister and First Lord
of the Treasury

Henrik Platou of Bergen told George Villiers in 1948 that this honour was awarded to:
Sylfest A. Myklatun, Gunnar Viveli, Sjur S. Hjølmo, Svein Kleivås, Lars L. Saebo, Lars Kvammen Viveli, Nils Olai Pedersen Storesund.

This certificate is awarded to

Mr Sylfest Anredsen Myklatun

as a token of gratitude for and appreciation of the help given to the Sailors, Soldiers and Airmen of the British Commonwealth of Nations, which enabled them to escape from, or evade capture by the enemy.

1939-1945

Air Chief Marshal,
Deputy Supreme Commander,
Allied Expeditionary Force

Decoration Recipients.
Svein Kleivkas, Sylfest Myklatun, Lars Saebo, Lars Myklatun, Sjur Hjølmo.

Reconstruction of the Escape Route

Translated from *På Flukt I Hardanger* the Norwegian edition of *Hiding in Hardanger*

Gunnar Strandenes of Bergen undertook to research the escape route of the Villiers and Stoddart families.

These researches have resulted in that the escape route can now be reconstructed, documented and drawn on a map. Gunnar Strandenes has often stayed in Eidfjord and learned of the escape of the Villiers family after the war, from what the local people had told him. Strandenes has also been in contact with the author Arnfinn Haga who has written about the round trip to Shetland.

The Escape Route

In the tense situation that ruled in Europe before the outbreak of the Second World War it was natural that the British Intelligence Service was very active.

In the summer of 1939 the British Admiralty sent some twenty British Naval Officers to several Norwegian towns to survey the shipping.

Among the eight officers that came to Bergen were Lt. Cdr. George Villiers and Paymaster Stoddart. Villiers had his wife Anne and their two children with him, and Stoddart was accompanied by his Russian wife.

When the Germans invaded Norway on the 9th April 1940, the

British officers feared to be taken as spies, and the two families, six people in all, fled in haste from Bergen.

Villiers and Stoddart, dressed in civilian clothes, left Strandgaten together with their wives and the children, and walked to Kalfaret, Fridalen and Inndalen to Paradis. Then they went further by car through Nesttun, Midttun, Gullbotn, Kvamskogen and down Tokagjelet to Norheimsund. There they went in to the Sandven Hotel, where Mrs. Sandven offered help.

For several days they stayed in Kvamskogen in a holiday cottage they rented from Mrs Sandven. They later returned to Norheimsund where they hid in a house within walking distance of the hotel.

Villiers sent messages through his Norwegian connections that they were attempting to escape from Norway and wished to get in touch with the British Navy. They hoped that the Royal Navy would come to Norway to rescue them.

In 1939 the Norwegian Navy had requisitioned the fjord boat *Haus* to patrol. M.S. *Haus* was under the command of Loytnant Bugge. He was now ordered to fetch the fugitives from Vikøy where the two families had arrived by lorry from Norheimsund.

The book relates (p. 79) that after a boat trip of about five hours, they came to a place that Mrs. Villiers in the English edition called 'Eslervik'. Investigations show that Captain Bugge and the *Haus* brought the fugitives to Dimmelsvik on the 18th April 1940. From Dimmelsvik they were taken by lorry to Kapteinsgården in Uskedal.

The fugitives thought that they had made radio contact with the British Navy, but the book tells us (p. 81) that the contact was in fact with a radio station that had fallen into German hands.

Instructions were given that the two officers Villiers and Stoddart should be issued with Norwegian identity papers, and with borrowed Norwegian naval uniforms they travelled to Rosendal and were photographed. While working on the reconstruction of the route, I met the photographer Leif Omvik in Rosendal, and found that he still had the photographs which were still held, together with the unpaid bill for 5 kroner!

In Kapteinsgården there was a skirmish between the Germans and the Norwegian Resistance on 20th April 1940. The confrontation is well described in the first volume of *Kampene i Norge* ('The Campaigns in Norway 1940') by Andreas Hauge.

After the shoot-out around Kapteinsgården was over, the six fled further on foot over to Uskedalen, following in the tracks of, and then joining, members of the Norwegian Armed Resistance, who were retreating over the mountains. In their company the fugitives came down to the West bank of the Matrefjord, and were ferried by rowing boat over to Indre Matre. There they met Kaptein Ulstrup who promised to help them further.

From Indre Matre they were taken by Andreas Kvandal's lorry to Sunde in Matre; from there they went further with Kaptein Ulstrup and his men by boat to Fjaera at the end of the Åkrafjord. From Fjaera they travelled further by bus to Odda. Here they said farewell to Kaptein Ulstrup.

The British were then taken by car from Odda to Øvre Eidfjord, where they stayed at the Eidfjord Guesthouse.

Late one night they walked up Hjølmodale to Hjolmo. From here they walked up the Hjølmoberget (mountain), and were hidden in an old stone hut in Djupsgjilet which lies a little below the peak of Hjolmoberget. They later moved to Tjukkaskog (a wood) and to Legene in the same area.

After several weeks' stay in these three places, they walked to Viveli, where they rested about an hour before the long journey, walking across Vedal and further to Erdal that lies by the fjord several kilometres from Lower Eidfjord. This was a walk of nearly twenty hours. The trek was particularly difficult and exhausting because the rivers were in flood.

From Erdal the journey continued by boat to Kinsarvik. From Kinsarvik they were taken by boat over the fjord, through Lukksund over the Bjørnefjord, out of the Korsfjord, through Goltasund and past Telavåg to Syltøy (Sylt Island) west of Møvik on Sotra.

From here they crossed the North Sea on the fishing boat *Sjøglimt* ('Sea Gleam') with Jakob Syltøy and Halvard Lønøy as crew.

'Sjøglimt' returned to Syltøy after a successful voyage.

Gunnar Strandenes 1998

The Norwegian author Arnfinn Haga added to this account in 1998.

'In a conversation with skipper Jakob Syltøy in Bergen on the 14th September 1978, he told me that in July 1940 he had journeyed over to Shetland with his boat *Sjøglimt*. He went there with several British people. Kristen Branum of Bergen knew of the events, and it was Wigand Larsen who had contacted Syltøy. Wigand Larsen was hunting for a boat. The leader of the British, Villiers, was a commander in the British Navy, as Syltøy understood. He had been stationed in Bergen before April 1940 and had "certainly something to do with the North Sea convoys" said Syltøy. He thought Villiers was a naval attaché.

'The British had come into the area through Kinsarvik. There they had taken to the fells and stayed in a hut. Jakob Syltøy and a friend had gone with a motor boat to look for them, but failed to make contact and had to return, unsuccessful. Several days later the British came to Syltøy in an "old wreck of a boat". They had found the way themselves.

'The British were Villiers and his wife and two children and an assistant and his wife. Syltøy understood that Wigand Larsen had come with them from Kinsarvik. The group waited several days on Syltøy island, waiting for another Englishman. This Englishman had been interned at the Rosenkrantz Hotel, but had escaped. This had been planned by Wigand Larsen and Kristen Branum. This man pretended to be an ordinary English sailor and the Germans believed him, but in reality he was also in the intelligence service.

'For the crossing to Shetland the engineer Halvard Lønøy joined Jakob Syltøy. Before the journey both Jakob Syltøy and the fugitives had generous help from the shopkeeper Nils Pedersen Storesund who provided fuel and provisions for the North Sea crossing. He also arranged for the fugitives to hide in a hut on Syltøy while they waited for the starting signal. *Sjøglimt* returned from Shetland after a successful voyage.'

George Villiers was promoted to Commander and later became well known on BBC radio and TV.

Anne was happy to return to her beloved Vane House and garden.

Janet became a teacher and was Head of Tormead Middle School for 21 years.

Many Years Later

Simon became a Major in the Royal Artillery and was Mentioned In Despatches.

Simon trying on his father's jersey (under protest!)

Rupert enjoyed retirement in naval uniform with medal ribbons.

Simon's three lovely children, Clive, Virginia and Moira.

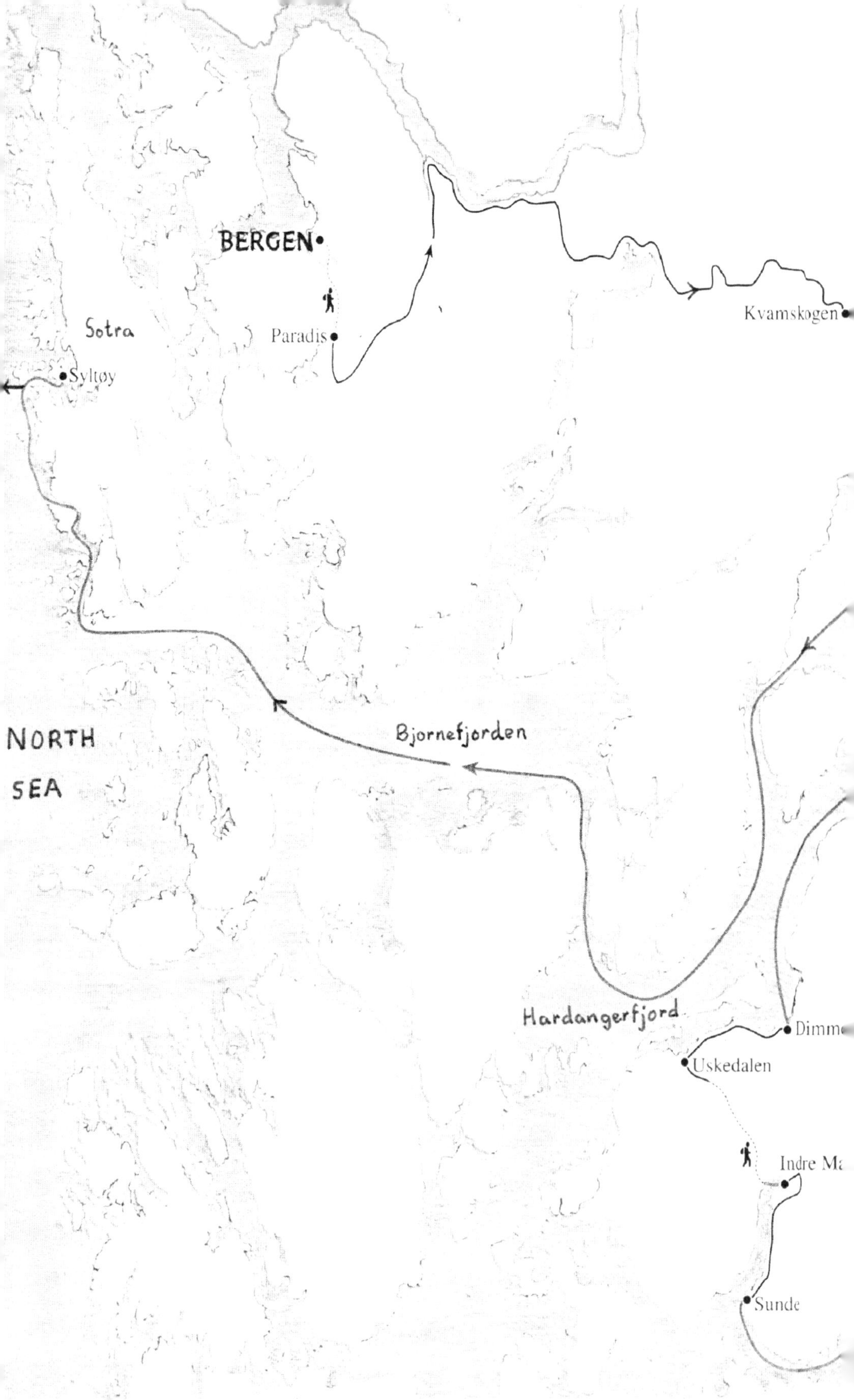
BERGEN
Paradis
Kvamskogen
Sotra
Syltøy
NORTH
SEA
Bjornefjorden
Hardangerfjord
Dimm
Uskedalen
Indre Ma
Sunde